LANGUAGE, SEX AND GENDER
DOES *LA DIFFÉRENCE* MAKE A DIFFERENCE?

ANNALS OF THE NEW YORK ACADEMY OF SCIENCES

Volume 327

LANGUAGE, SEX AND GENDER
DOES *LA DIFFÉRENCE* MAKE A DIFFERENCE?

Edited by Judith Orasanu, Mariam K. Slater, and Leonore Loeb Adler

The New York Academy of Sciences
New York, New York
1979

Library of Congress Cataloging in Publication Data

Main entry under title:

Language, sex, and gender.

(Annals of the New York Academy of Sciences; v. 327)
Papers presented at a workshop sponsored by the Anthropology, Linguistics, and Psychology Sections of the New York Academy of Sciences held Oct. 22, 1977.
Bibliography: p.
1. Language and languages—Sex differences—Congresses. I. Orasanu, Judith. II. Slater, Mariam. III. Adler, Leonore Loeb. IV. New York Academy of Sciences. Section of Anthropology. V. New York Academy of Sciences. Section of Linguistics. VI. New York Academy of Sciences. Section of Psychology. VII. Series: New York Academy of Sciences. Annuals; v. 327.
Q11.N5 vol. 327 [P120.S48] 508'.1s [301.2'1] 79–14741

KG/CCP
Printed in the United States of America
ISBN 0-89766-022-6

ANNALS OF THE NEW YORK ACADEMY OF SCIENCES

VOLUME 327

LANGUAGE, SEX AND GENDER:
DOES *LA DIFFÉRENCE* MAKE A DIFFERENCE?*

June 25, 1979

Editors

JUDITH ORASANU, MARIAM K. SLATER, AND LEONORE LOEB ADLER

CONTENTS

* The papers in this volume are the result of a workshop entitled Language, Sex, and Gender: Does "la Différence" Make a Difference? that was held on October 22, 1977, and sponsored by the Anthropology, Linguistics, and Psychology Sections of the New York Academy of Sciences.

INTRODUCTION

Judith Orasanu

Laboratory of Experimental Psychology
The Rockefeller University
New York, New York 10021

Mariam K. Slater

Department of Anthropology
Queens College, City University of New York
Flushing, New York 11367

Graduate Center, City University of New York
New York, New York 10036

Leonore Loeb Adler

Department of Psychology
The College of Staten Island, City University of New York
Staten Island, New York 10301

A sexual dichotomy marks many if not all species. Humans, being human, express many of the differences in linguistic codes or messages. In the Indo-European family, this interface between social reality and verbal expression is a matter that was formally recognized at least by the time of the Greeks, as illustrated by Gregersen in this volume. More recently, the latest form of feminism has brought the interface front and center. One attempt to resolve some of the problems raised by feminist issues was published in McGraw Hill's 1974 guidelines for equal treatment of the sexes.

Extremes in the range of responses were printed in Letters to the *New York Times* (1974). Implicit in them are attitudes to whether English is a sexist language or not, and if so, whether reform is possible. One pole was represented by a female instructor in architecture at Pratt Institute (Mimi Lobell):

> It is no accident that the male became the accepted model of humanity, yet I suspect that the main reaction to . . . [suggested reform] will be, "What difference does it make?" Speaking as a woman, it makes all the difference in the world. Using terms like *mankind* instead of *humankind* leaves me and all other women out of the human race. It conjures up . . . images of being kept veiled and secluded, "barefoot and pregnant . . ."

The opposite pole is represented by a University of Chicago letter writer, a linguist (James McCawley), who for reasons expanded in Gregersen's paper claims that language reform only exacerbates a social problem, and that a linguistic problem is nonexistent. In scholarly articles, one also sees contradictory evidence. For example, women often felt that *he* and *him* excluded them (Bem and Bem, 1973). However, an earlier wave of feminism ridiculed such phrases as, "Is there a doctoress in the house?" as invidious.

Clearly, we must ask, to whom and to what does *la différence* make a difference? *La différence* in our title refers to a popular tag line in Western folklore. A debate among French cabinet ministers about the equality and fraternity (*sic*) of females and males ends with the following celebratory shout: "*Vive la différence!*" Even this biological and hormonal dichotomy has become more of a continuum as genetic drift as well as surgery justify the following headline, which described John Napier's predictions of unisex somatic changes that are taking place: "It's Getting Tougher to Tell the Difference."

Before we introduce the concept of "difference" that derives from structural linguistics, let us point out that all languages provide options in the pragmatic manner by which a particular meaning is expressed, whatever the formal grammar prescribes. Sex or gender groups may differ in their selection among those options, as suggested by Lakoff (this volume). Identification of those differences in any systematic way is only beginning (see Frank, 1978 for a recent review), and the significance of those differences remains to be established. Sociolinguistic research (Gumperz, 1971) indicates that inferences are drawn about social roles and statuses on the basis of speech, and those differences undoubtedly influence the treatment accorded the speaker.

Because of the current interest in these issues, a workshop on the relation among the variables mentioned in our title seemed appropriate for a joint sponsorship by the Anthropology, Linguistics, and Psychology sections of The New York Academy of Sciences. We tried to provide diverse approaches by inviting participants from several disciplines for the one-day symposium.

In the first paper, Edgar Gregersen, an anthropologist and linguist, provides an overview of the issues addressed by the other participants. In addition to presenting his own research on curses used by males in more than 100 cultures, he examines evidence bearing on the Sapir-Whorf hypothesis in cultures that have undergone extreme social change and/or language change. In the second paper, Edward Bendix, another anthropological linguist, also addresses the Sapir-Whorf hypothesis, but through a theoretical linguistic analysis of possible meanings of the pronoun "he." The third paper by John Beatty, also an anthropological linguist, involves a semantic analysis of sex (biologically defined), roles (as in social interaction), and sex roles (as involved in sexual behavior). Examples from American, Japanese, and Mohawk languages and culture are examined for what they express about the relation between language and social categories, including homosexual patterns.

The remaining three papers deal with differences in various aspects of language *use* by females and males. Robin Lakoff, a generative linguist, extends the theory of generative transformational grammar (à la Chomsky) to an explication of sex difference in style, primarily language style. She considers implications of that theory for understanding cross-sex misunderstandings. Candace West, a sociologist, addresses the issue of whether women "ask for" the kind of treatment they frequently receive from men through an analysis of overlaps or interruptions in cross-sex conversations and responses to these interruptions. In the last paper, Adelaide Haas, a speech pathologist, examines the development of "gender-lect," or sex-associated features of speech, in young children. The discussant, Jessie Bernard, a sociologist, brought her experience in sex-related research to bear in her comments. Taken together, these papers contribute to our understanding of the contexts in which gender-marked features of speech, whether semantic, syntactic or pragmatic, make a difference and the implications of those differences for social realities.

The notion of "difference," as mentioned above, is also applicable to the present symposium in yet a further way. In linguistics, the notion of difference, meaning *contrast*, is employed at many levels in the scientific analysis of sound and meaning systems. The systematic nature of a language at a given time—its *structure*—was referred to by the pioneer in modern scientific linguistics, Ferdinand de Saussure (1916), as *langue* as distinguished from *parole*. The latter refers to speech acts in their concrete forms. Noam Chomsky calls this distinction competence as opposed to utterance, and philosophers have for centuries separated the type from the token, cat-ness as opposed to cat[1], cat[2], . . . In this volume, the effect of *langue* and *parole* on each other is one of the questions raised by some of the discussion of pronoun reference and the organization of lexical and syntactic items pertaining to various sex/gender groups (cf. Beatty and Bendix).

In its broadest frame, the relation between linguistic and social reality first developed by Edward Sapir and Benjamin Lee Whorf is addressed by such questions. The debate over the Sapir-Whorf hypothesis—that language actually molds thought rather than merely reflecting it—has now been drawn into the arena of sexual politics with which our introduction began. Whorfianism is interpreted by some to apply solely to structural features of language, and by others, to pragmatic aspects as well.

Not only the notion of structural differences, but also the concept of gender is common to studies of sex roles and language. Sex refers to a combination of genetic and/or hormonal aspects of a person's identity, and gender refers in recent studies of sex roles to the social or cultural categorization of individuals whose sex is sometimes irrelevant to the person's role. For example, in certain Plains Indian cultures of North America, a male called a *berdache* is accorded the role of a women (Devereux, 1937). The *berdache* is expected to marry another genetic male, but the gender of the *berdache* is female. Among the topics discussed by Beatty, the linguistic reflection of homosexuality is explored. Gender, as Bendix points out, does not only refer to the categories created by reproductive differences—male/female and their representation in grammar as masculine/feminine—but also to other syntactic structurings. Gender basically means category, and sexual ones provide only a few of them. The Bantu languages, for example, have some 15 genders, including animate, inanimate, and the like.

To summarize, this collection of papers throws light on a series of questions raised in many disciplines. The arbitrary connection between sex and gender was first systematically explored by Margaret Mead in *Sex and Temperament in Three Primitive Societies* (1935). We hope that this volume will extend the work such explorations began.

REFERENCES

BEM, S.L. & D.J. BEM. 1973. Does sex-biased job advertising "aid and abet" sex discrimination? Journal of Applied Social Psychology 3:6–18.
DE SAUSSURE, F. 1916. Cours de Linguistique Générale. Paris: Payot. (English translation 1959, New York: Philosophical Library)
DEVEREUX, G. 1937. Institutionalized homosexuality of the Mohave Indians. Human Biology 9:498–527.
FRANK, F.W. 1978. Women's language in America. *In* Women's Language and Style. D. Butturff & E.L Epstein, Eds. Studies in Contemporary Language, No. 1. Department of English, University of Akron. Akron, Ohio.
GUMPERZ, J. 1971. Language in Social Groups. Stanford, Ca.: Stanford University Press.
LOBELL, M. 1974. Letters. The New York Times, Nov. 10, A22.
MCCAWLEY, J. 1974. Letters. The New York Times, Nov. 10, A22.
MEAD, M. 1935. Sex and Temperament in Three Primitive Societies. New York: William Morrow.
NAPIER, J. 1966. The New York World-Telegram and Sun, Mar. 11.

Abstract

SEXUAL LINGUISTICS

EDGAR GREGERSEN

As keynote speaker, Gregersen gives an overview of the topics covered in the conference, and also summarizes the results of his own research on cross-cultural swearing patterns. As an anthropological linguist, he also offers a comparative sampling of cases showing that women's status and structural features of language co-vary independently. The relevance of such matters to political issues raised by the women's movement is emphasized, and wherever examples from other disciplines are available, they are considered.

More than 100 languages are represented in Gregersen's survey of swearing. Informants attest to the fact that swearing itself is frequently an aspect of male style, reflecting the dominance and deference acted out in the culture.

The content of the curses often contains sexual slurs. Even the words for a woman, as Muriel Schulz has shown (1975), begin as neutral terms, but are likely to become pejorative. Consider *madam* and *mistress* as opposed to *sir* and *master*. In minority politics as well as sexual politics, ideologically progressive terms can accompany hostile emotions.

Not only group relations, but also family relations are reflected in sexual linguistic patterns. About two-thirds of the languages in the cursing sample (66 out of 103) consider the worst abuse to be a derogatory reference to the opponent's mother.

To suggest language reform in order to alter social realities requires belief that fundamental social structures and their psychological impact will give way by fiat. Whether the data come from psychology or comparative and theoretical linguistics, the question of reform addresses the validity of the Whorfian hypothesis. Whorfianism expresses the notion that categories of language will determine, influence, or at least correlate consistently with perceptions of the nonlinguistic world. It is difficult to see, he says, how speaking a language in itself makes one sexist, whatever the grammatical forms. The charge, he continues, would make sense only in two ways: First, some forms are called sexist by fiat whether or not any correspondence with the real world exists. Secondly, linguistic formulas are sexist because they correlate with the subordinate position of women in a given society, and because they contribute to maintaining the situation. The first criterion of sexism equates a given symbol with a political attitude, which may in turn indicate power. However, whether such power is socially significant is another matter, and one that he does not analyze. Regarding the second measure of sexism, however, Gregersen offers a number of negative examples of the Whorfian hypothesis. He takes his data from a wide variety of languages and societies—Norway, China, Turkey, Russia, Luo, Mohawk—which show that social order and the aspects of language in question would seem to vary independently. The features touched on pertain to suggestions for escaping "androcentric" pronoun agreement, on the one hand, and the general proposal by linguistic reformers that terms cannot simultaneously function as generic and specific entities.

Editors

SEXUAL LINGUISTICS

Edgar A. Gregersen

Department of Anthropology, Queens College, City University of New York
Flushing, New York 11367

Graduate Center, City University of New York
New York, New York 10036

The Women's Movement raised the issue of sexism in language as a political issue. In so doing, it has prompted a reconsideration of the topics of sex and gender in their relation to linguistics, and more generally of dominance and deference as revealed by linguistic behavior. In this conference, we shall examine a number of these topics, all of which I subsume under the label of "sexual linguistics."

The original charge of sexism was accompanied by a number of demands for language reform. Some of these reforms have gained considerable acceptance within the English language community, but although this acceptance in and of itself is of great interest sociolinguistically, most of what will be said today will be concerned not so much with prescriptive matters as with other, more theoretical issues. One of these is, the question of how sex is conceptualized in linguistic terms to begin with. It would be interesting to find out how members of deviant sex groups deal with such matters—not only homosexuals, transvestites, and transsexuals, but also a relatively recent group in American society that has been referred to in the literature as "radical drag" but in the group itself is called "gender fuck" (bearded transvestites are the most notable examples of this phenomenon).[1] Unfortunately, there is no discussion of such groups in the present workshop.

Three basic nonprescriptive areas have developed within sexual linguistics: (1) how are sex and gender designated in a language? (2) how do the members of the two sexes actually speak? and (3) how do they acquire whatever linguistic differences they use? In this volume, a number of topics in these areas will be considered in original contributions. I see my own function as summarizing the kinds of work done previously or as highlighting various topics to be discussed later on by the other authors. My own relevance for the conference comes in part from a project I am currently engaged in: a cross-cultural study of cursing and abuse, which really relates to all three areas of interest. Curiously enough, one of the earliest practical examples recorded of a difference between the way men and women speak has to do with swearing. In Aristophanes' play *The Ecclesiazuae* (393 B.C.), a woman is going to pose as a man as part of a plot for women to take over

---

[1] See in particular the work of Laud Humphries.

0077-8923/79/0327-0003 $01.75/2 ©1979, NYAS

the government. She makes a slip by swearing "By the two goddesses!" [Demeter and Persephone]: mà tò θe 5η [μὰ τῶν θεῶν]. This was apparently the favorite oath of Athenian women. Ancient Greek men apparently never swore by goddesses at all, only by gods. The scene is sufficiently interesting to warrant quoting it more fully.

PRAXAGORA: Try to speak worthily, let your language be truly manly, and lean on your staff with dignity.

FIRST WOMAN: [who is trying to imitate a man while rehearsing her speech] I had rather have seen one of your regular orators giving you wise advice: but, as that is not to be, it behooves me to break silence; I cannot, for my part indeed, allow the tavern-keepers to fill up their wine-pits with water. No, by the two goddesses . . .

PRAXAGORA: What? by the two goddesses! Wretched woman, where are your senses?

FIRST WOMAN: Eh! what? . . . I have not asked you for a drink.

PRAXAGORA: No, but you want to pass for a man, and your swear by the two godesses. Otherwise you did very well.

FIRST WOMAN: Well then. By Apollo . . .

PRAXAGORA: Stop! All these details of language must be adjusted; else it is quite useless to go to the Assembly. [lines 149-162][2]

In my own study involving more than 100 languages from all the continents and representing many different evolutionary stages of society, it is clear that swearing is generally considered a man's style, that in no society are women supposed to be more prolific or serious cursers than men—the Billingsgate fishwife notwithstanding—, and that it may be the case that women swear considerably less often or less violently than men. Robin Lakoff, in *Language and Woman's Place* (1975), has suggested that swearing plays a significant role in male bonding and that swearing somehow makes the swearer be taken seriously. I am not sure that merely adopting swearing as a style would radically change the social position of women. There are societies in which women apparently swear the same way men do, but overt institutional power resides with the men, as in virtually all (if not all) societies.

In some of the following sections, I shall refer to specific insults found in various societies. In order to retain the flavor of the original expression, I have used comparable English words.

As an example of the difference between the swearing practices of men and women, consider the Gurindji of Northern Australia. In some feminist literature, the hunting and gathering level of human economic evolution seems to be equated with a kind of sexual egalitarian golden age. The Gurindji, who are hunters and gatherers, fail to meet this vision. Their worst possible set insult is to say to a man "you stinking prick." Among men, this utterance in fairly common—and it is only occasionally that

---

[2] The translation is from the edition by Benjamin Bickley Rogers, London: George Bell & Sons, 1902.

violence will erupt because of it. But for a woman to say it to a man is instant disaster: she would be speared with no questions asked (at least in the old days). On the other hand, for a man to swear in the presence of women is bad, and especially shocking in the presence of his mother-in-law.[3]

A related topic is what terms of abuse are directed to women as opposed to men. Muriel Schulz, in her paper, "The semantic derogation of women"[4] has marshalled a considerable amount of evidence to show that an originally innocent term for a woman frequently becomes pejorative, usually a sexual slur. The same is seldom true for comparable terms denoting men. For example, from English we find *Madam* and *Mistress* as opposed to *Sir* and *Master*. To call a man a "professional" may be quite different from calling a woman one. In French, *fille* (originally simply "daughter, girl") so often means "prostitute" that one must usually say *jeune fille* literally "young girl" in nonpejorative senses. There is no comparable ambivalence about *fils* "son." Schulz concludes by noting that such pejoration "both reflects and perpetuates derogatory attitudes toward women," and insists that it be "abjured" (p. 73). I must say I find it difficult to see how such developments can be controlled by fiat. Although it is no doubt therapeutic to raise one's own self image by whatever way possible, nevertheless, a mere change of label brings about short-term relief only. Ideologically correct terms can accompany the most odious and hostile of sentiments, and it is the sentiments that count in the long run. For sentiments to change, the social reality must probably change first—although there is an admitted feedback that complicates any analysis.

A dramatic example of the difficulties involved in trying to get a better self image through change of label came across to me in a men's room at my university. This room had particularly extensive graffiti expressing a variety of political and other opinions drawn in technicolor magic marker. It was a veritable Sistine Chapel of verbal abuse. On one wall was scribbled "Kill all

---

[3] I am indebted to Patrick McConvell for this information.

[4] Included in BARRIE THORN and NANCY HENLEY, Eds., 1975, *Language and Sex: Difference and Dominance,* Newbury House, Rowley. This collection is invaluable not only for the articles it includes but also for its summary of the recent literature. For a valuable bibliography on earlier and essentially non-English materials, see Carlo Tagliavini, 1936, Modificazioni del linguaggio nella parlata delle donne, in *Scritti in onere di Alfredo Trombetti,* Milano (pp. 82-146); and Hernando Balmori (date?), Habla mujeril, *Filología,* Buenos Aires **8**:123-138. Other more recent articles written from an essentially feminist perspective include: J DE STEFANO. 1977, *Sex differences in language: a cross national perspective with emphasis on English* (paper presented at the International Studies Association meeting, St. Louis); L. HARRISON. 1975. Cro-Magnon woman—in eclipse, *The Science Teacher* **42**:8-11; L. HARRISON & R. PASSERO. 1975. Sexism in the language in the elementary textbooks, *Science and Children* **128**: 22-25; V. KIDD. 1971. A study of the images produced through the use of the male pronoun as the generic, *Moments in Contemporary Rhetoric and Communication* **1**:25-30; J. SCHNEIDER & S. HACKER. 1973. Sex role imagery and the use of the generic 'man' in introductory texts: a case in the sociology of sociology, *American Sociologist* **8**:12-18; M. J. SCHNEIDER & K. A. FOSS. 1977. Thought, sex and language; the Sapir-Whórf hypothesis in the American women's movement, *Bulletin: Women's Studies in Communication* **1**:1-7; WENDY MARTYNA. 1978. What does 'he' mean? Use of the generic masculine, Journal of Communication **28**:131-138

blacks"; on the other, "Kill all gays." In a sense, it would have been less disturbing if the inscriptions read "Kill all niggers" and "Kill all faggots." But in any event, it is clear that the recent ameliorative labels that have been pushed by the Black and homosexual liberation movements have, at least for some speakers, in turn become pejorative already.

I suggest that some of the issues we are dealing with involve psychological problems that even a rationally organized society would have a hard time to escape.

Abuse reserved for an opponent's mother is a case in point. Not that mothers are held in contempt—on the contrary, it seems that all societies clearly recognize the enormous importance of mothers. More and more data suggest that the role of mother in the lives of their children is awesome, and that people with not-good-enough mothers (a technical notion) may be greatly hampered in their psychosexual adjustment. Interestingly enough, of the 103 languages I have cursing information on, 66 consider as their gravest insult and abuse a curse directed at the opponent's mother. Al Goldstein, the infamous publisher of *Screw* magazine, has said that as a child growing up in the jungles of Brooklyn, the only way he could survive was to become a masterful "mother-mocker."[5] We are all familiar with the American English expression *mother fucker* (originally restricted to Blacks and possibly African in origin). But I can think of no comparable expression involving father; surely "your father's moustache" and "so's your old man" do not fit the emotional bill. In the recent film, *The Exorcist,* the most shocking thing the scriptwriters could think up for the demonically possessed girl to say was a new mother insult: "Your mother sucks cocks in hell." (When I saw the movie, the audience reaction to this was mixed: some people groaned; others giggled; one voice was heard saying, "Well, hell can't be all that bad then.") Other imaginative insults of this kind can be found. I recently saw (on another men's room wall at school) the following: "Your mother has 47 pubic hairs. I counted them last night."

Cross-culturally, mother insults are quite varied. I list a few of these below. Possibly the most frequent set insult in the world is "your mother's cunt." This is found in Arabic, Indonesian, Fijian, Thai, Swahili, Xhosa, Ambo, Wolof, Cuban Spanish, and Serbo-Croatian. Other insults include:

I will tear apart your mother's cunt (Sango [Central African Empire])
I will fuck your mother (Amharic, Armenian, Bulgarian, Burmese, Dinka [Sudan], Fulani [Mali])
You are your mother's cunt (Malagasy)
Son of a cunt with pus in it (or) Son of a cunt with gravel in it (Nama Hottentot)
Your mother fucks dogs (Lao)
Fuck your stinking whore of a mother (Hungarian)

---

[5] This was in a radio interview which I believe occurred in the summer of 1977 on a New York City station.

Go to the whore who gave you birth (Spanish)
I shit in the milk of your mother (Spanish)
Your old mother's stinking milk (Cantonese)
You eat your mother's menstrual blood (Enga [New Guinea])
Fucker of your mother's cunt (Hindi)
Fuck your mother (Turkish, Ponapean, Haitian Creole)
I fuck you in the ass on your mother (Rumanian)
You come from the devil's cunt-hole (Guarani [Paraguay])
I fuck your old mother's broken down stinking cunt (Cantonese).

I have not considered here insults on the order of "bastard," which might be considered a kind of mother insult.

Only twenty languages of the sample have father insults; and of these five have father insults that are not considered as being particularly awful. An insult to a father almost invariably presupposes the existence of an insult to a mother (there are only two exceptions to this in my sample). Father insults are fairly unimaginative, being usually "your father's prick" or "father fucker." Malay has an unusual one: "lick up your father's semen." In Sango, an insult occurs that I would have classified as a mother insult, but my informant counted it as a father insult: "your mother's cunt is dry." It is an insult against one's father, it was argued, because it means that your father is impotent and hence cannot lubricate your mother's vagina. But clearly, there is nothing that even remotely approaches the virtuosity involved in producing mother insults. In fact, verbal abuse directed against mothers is so common that the traditional word for "mother" has itself occasionally become obscene. Thus, throughout the Spanish-speaking world the expression *tu madre* "your mother" suffices as a grave insult in its own right. Consequently, *mamá* is frequently substituted in nonobscene situations. The English word *mother* (pronounced *móder*) is used instead in some parts of Mexico. The same sort of thing has happened in Xhosa, a language spoken in southern Africa—but here, interestingly enough, the old word for "father" has undergone the same substitution.

Quite obviously, we find here serious instances of pejoration. But simply to take the view that "it is an insult to women to insult mothers and so stop it" misses all the psychological implications of the unique and probably necessary role of mothers in the lives of both sons and daughters. One of my informants (for Umbundu, spoken in Angola) was a man who had fought the Portuguese in guerrilla skirmishes, had been detained in prisons, and had confronted top politicians of both the communist and capitalist worlds. He readily gave me the cursing information I sought, including the most terrible set insult in his language: "Your mother from whom blood oozes out." When asked if I could use his name in the published version of my study, he said "of course." But some minutes later he changed his mind because, he said, he was afraid his *mother* might find out about it. His mother was illiterate and could not speak English. Even for a revolutionary, mothers can be terrifying. If the Western ideal of masculinity is an intolerable burden for men, so the requirements of motherhood must be appallingly difficult for women—and for their children. The curses of the world bear this out.

Studies of how the sexes are designated in languages are often couched in terms of the Whorfian hypothesis, even though this is usually not stated. And this is of some consequence because, ever since the Chomskyan revolution in linguistics, it becomes increasingly difficult to take the general Whorfian position seriously. At least some parts of the feminist linguistic critique must, therefore, be rejected if the larger Whorfian hypothesis is rejected, which I think it must be.

Statements about "sexist" *he* or *man* in English are usually totally within the naïve Whorfian tradition, to the effect that the categories of language will determine, influence, or at least be correlated with the perceptions of the real world. Thus, it has been alleged that since the standard literary English construction such as *mankind, the science of man* [= anthropology], *everyone . . . he,* or *the doctor . . . his* use a masculine form generically, speakers of English will share expectations that only men count or only men will become doctors. In line with this sort of thinking, Marvin Harris changed the title of his anthropology text from *Culture, Man, Nature,* to *Culture, People, Nature* in the second edition. The American Anthropological Association in its annual *Guide to Departments of Anthropology* changed its designation for a head of a department from *chairman* to *chairperson* in its 1975-1976 edition.

The *Newsletter of the American Anthropological Association* in 1972 saw a fairly lively correspondence about sexist language, some of it from men who were clearly trying to ridicule the linguistic purification feminists were demanding. The first in the series was from Ann Bodine (1972, April). She wrote:

> Please let's stop using sexist expressions such as that in the January 1972 *Newsletter . . . :* "Eleanor Leacock for a 2-year term established to effect transition to a *9-man* (!!!!) Board."

Bodine subsequently did a study of another "sexist" construction, viz., the use of *he* to refer to *anyone, someone,* etc. She counseled in this later paper that the colloquial use of *they* rather than *he* was ideologically acceptable.

In the same issue of the *Newsletter* (1972, April), Paul Kay acerbically suggested the creation of a new third person pronoun for English to refer to human referents regardless of sex. The form he proposes is [mf] (pronounced /emef/), derived from "male-female"; I wonder if this is not a tongue-in-cheek reference to the book by Anthony Burgess which had appeared the year before (1971): *M/F,* the title of which stands for *motherfucker.* Kay is quite willing to go along with [fm], however, and says in the closing line of his letter: "The issue could . . . be put to the membership in the form of a mail—sorry, postal ballot." Here we also find an instance of linguistic avoidance (i.e. shunning *mail* because it sounds the same as *male*) to rival the most conservative Zulu *hlonipa.* I presume Kay is joking.

Two months later (1972, June), Robert B. Kaplan suggested yet another common gender pronoun with the following forms: *shis* "he/she," *shim* "him/her," *shim(s)* "his/her(s)," *shimself* "himself/herself."

By December of the same year, the editorial board of the *Newsletter* found it necessary to stop letters about sexist language. The last one printed was by Jane Mobley Miller who felt the expressions *science of man, primitive man, early man, origin of man,* and the like were offensive to women, and implored: "Let's rid ourselves of these sexist words before we raise another generation of sexist anthropologists."

In all honesty, it is difficult to see how speaking a language in itself makes one sexist, whatever grammatical or lexical forms one uses. It seems to me that there are only two ways in which a charge of sexism would make any sense. (1) Certain linguistic formulas are simply branded as sexist by fiat, whether or not any correlation with the status of women in the real world can be demonstrated or not. In short, "sexist" *he* or *man* is a symbol: people in favor of women's liberation should avoid them and use other forms simply because doing so would point to allegiance to the cause. Edward Bendix discusses this point in his paper. As a matter of fact, the eradication of "sexist" constructions *would* probably indicate that the movement had considerable power. But whether it would be power that mattered is another question. (2) Certain linguistic formulas are sexist because they can be correlated with the subordinate position of women in a society and contribute to keeping women subordinate. This is a matter for empirical verification. As far as I can see, the studies that have attempted to provide such verification are exceedingly weak and often evince a petty over-empiricism rather than more satisfactory strategies of explanation. (see Thorne and Henley, 1975; Harrison, 1975a and 1975b; Kidd, 1971; Schneider and Hocker, 1973; Schneider and Foss, 1977: more interesting is Martyna 1978 [cf. note 4 for bibliographical details.])

Consider the issue of generic *he* in English. Bodine's suggestion is, as we have seen, to substitute *they* or something similar for what she calls the "androcentric" agreement. In my own natural informal speech this is what I generally do to begin with, and I notice a great many other people do the same thing whatever their position on the women's movement. Joseph F. Foster points out that in the Ozark Mountain Dialect of English (spoken in the mountain areas of Arkansas, Missouri, and Oklahoma), *they* is invariably used to agree with *somebody, child, beaver,* etc., but that native speakers of this dialect "are highly unlikely to be among those people sympathetic to anti-sexist movements." He concludes that if this is in fact the case, "one might infer that despite wishes to the contrary, language and social organization are really distinct orders of phenomena" (Newsletter, AAA, 1972, June, p. 4).

Foster's position is supported by the cross-cultural data. Languages without overt sex differences in pronouns (e.g. Luo, and East African Nilotic language, uses εn where English distinguishes *he/she/it*)—and these are the great majority of languages in the world at present—are associated with social structures having markedly different roles for men and women. The classic example of this is Turkish, which for centuries until the formation of the Turkish Republic in 1923 was spoken in a society with an enormous difference in the social status of men and women, in part characterized by the fact that women had to wear veils in public, had to observe other rules of decorum separating them from men (purdah), were not educated and could not enter any of the professions except prostitution. Men could have up to four wives and many concubines, and divorce their wives at will; reciprocal rights for women did not exist. The same things were of course true of other Islamic societies, notably the Arabic-speaking groups that had sex gender in pronouns. When Turkish society changed, the pronoun system did not change with it. What can we conclude from this? That sex gender in pronouns is irrelevant for social structure and the life chances and expectations of men and women. The "feminist" notion of sexist vs. nonsexist languages reminds mé of the Russian linguist Marr who asserted that there were Communist vs. non-Communist languages. This became the party line in the Soviet Union until no less a linguist than Stalin himself demolished it by pointing out that Russian before the 1917 Revolution was the same as the Russian spoken after it. (For a discussion of Marr, see R. H. Robins, 1972, *A Short History of Linguistics,* Bloomington: Indiana University Press p. 225.)

As a matter of fact, the Russian situation has direct relevance for the present discussion. Recall the lament that the English construction "Every doctor should do his duty" may indoctrinate speakers with the expectation that only men can become doctors. A similar construction occurs in Russian with unmarked nouns denoting professions that both men and women belong to, as for example *vrač* [врач] "physician, doctor." As Robert Rothstein has pointed out in his article "Sex, Gender and the October Revolution" (1973), most of the professions—including medicine—were not open to women in Russia before 1917. After the revolution, the professions were opened—but without previous linguistic conditioning. That is, *vrač* did not undergo some anticipatory demasculinization to entice women to become doctors. At the present day, the majority of doctors in the Soviet Union are in fact women. But in speaking about doctors in general, masculine agreements are still used, and this is most commonly done even with reference to a specific woman doctor; thus, *stárij vrač ušól* [старый врач ушёл] "the old doctor left" refers to either a man or a woman. The agreements are masculine both for the adjective (*stárij* "old") and the verb (*ušól* "left"). To refer to women, two other constructions are possible, but less frequent. The one gaining the most ground has the verb showing feminine agreement, but the adjective remains masculine: *stárij vrač ušlá* [старый врач ушла]. The least common of all constructions is to make all the agreements feminine: *stáraja vrač ušlá* [старая врач ушла]. Here we are talking not about general statements but about reference to a specific woman!

It might be argued that we have been dealing with societies that are patri-oriented, or have shown a consistent patri-bias in their history. What about societies that are matri-oriented? Don't such things as agreements behave in exactly the opposite way to what we have just seen? In other words, should we not find a mirror image, with feminine pronouns, and so on, in the fore? To a limited extent we do, but not entirely so. The prime example in the literature is Mohawk, considered in some detail by John Beatty elsewhere in this volume. Mohawk society is matrilocal, matrilineal, with succession to political office through women. Linguistically, the interesting thing is that there is an indefinite pronoun that is feminine in form. But elsewhere in the grammar female "sexist" language conventions are dropped. For example, the pronouns have masculine and feminine forms for the third person dual and plural (i.e., *they* plural masculine, *they* plural feminine). There is no common gender plural. In referring to a mixed group of men and women, the masculine forms are always used—even if there is only one man and a hundred women. This, even in a society with perhaps the highest status accorded to women anywhere. (It must be conceded, however, that even among the Mohawk, the highest overt power remains in the hands of men, though it is legitimized through women.)

The feminist linguistic critique, such as it is, is to play down special words for women as opposed to men, including pronouns. Interestingly enough, there are at least two languages where within the past century such distinctions have been played up. These languages are Norwegian and Chinese. A marvelously ridiculous case can be made for correlating the improved social position women have gained in Norway and China with these linguistic changes. Literary Norwegian until the turn of the century made use of two gender system (common/neuter) as in Danish and Swedish, rather than the original Old Norse three (masculine/feminine/neuter), which had been preserved in local dialects. By a series of parliamentary decrees, the feminine gender was reintroduced into the language, and a 1938 language reform made the feminine form obligatory for about 1000 nouns. Nationalism rather than feminism was the motivation for the change: the feminine gender was felt to be a particularly Norwegian linguistic trait. The movement to restore this trait occurred virtually simultaneously with the improvement of the social status of women, including women's suffrage and various other political and economic changes. But the correlation is ridiculous because the same changes occurred in Denmark and Sweden where the linguistic situation was different. In passing, we might note that the Danish common gender forms are historically masculine, whereas a great many of the Swedish common gender forms are historically feminine (e.g. *denna* "this" is the common gender form, originally feminine, that has virtually ousted the masculine *denne* except in formal style). Even so, the social developments have been the same in all three countries.

An even more farfetched example is presented by Chinese. In spoken Chinese (Mandarin), there is no gender in pronouns; thus tā as it is written in Pin-yin (phonetically /thá/), the official romanization, means "he/she/it." In the traditional logographic writing system, only a single character for tā was used: 他. About the time of the 1917 Literary Revolution in China, a special character was developed to correspond to "she/her" found in European languages: 她. The original character was thereby redefined as "he/him." But in the spoken language, no change at all occurred. The form of the new pronoun was arrived at by dropping the left-hand segment of the original pronoun, 亻, which is the radical for "man, person," and substituting the radical for "woman": 女. The motivation for creating the new character was probably ease in translating the great masses of European texts that flooded China. Yet another pronoun for "it" was created, but is seldom used: 牠 (or in a variant form, 它), where the first part of the character is the radical for "animal": 牜 [this "it" refers only to nonhuman animates; inanimates require another pronoun, tō not tā].[6] But some writers went further and adopted a special feminine form for nǐ "you singular," the original character for "you" being redefined as "you masculine": 你 "you singular masculine" (originally "you singular"), 妳 "you singular feminine." No European languages except Basque (in some inflections) make this distinction and it is rare among the languages of the world, though it does exist, e.g. in Hausa and Arabic.

The social correlates that could be suggested are many, and include the abolition of foot-binding, the outlawing of polygyny and concubinage, the massive rehabilitation of prostitutes, along with woman's suffrage, and so on. But not even the most convinced Whorfian would probably want to take up this line, particularly since we are dealing merely with changes in the writing system, not with the real language. Nevertheless, the correlations I have offered here are more substantial than anything that has been used to bolster the feminist position on sexist pronouns.

The feminist assault on the generic use of *man* has about the same validity as the attack on indefinite *he,* it seems to me. But it is more insidious because it attacks a general feature of English and perhaps all other languages in the world, viz., that a noun may have both a generic and specific use. I remember well an extraordinary discussion I had with an aunt of mine when I was about ten years old. She was a native speaker of Norwegian and her knowledge of English—though adequate—was imperfect. One day she asked me how long a "day" was. I was surprised at the question because I thought she knew. I said, twenty-four hours. Then she asked, but don't a day and a night add to twenty-four hours. I said yes. She got very angry with me and said that I shouldn't try to fool her just because she was a foreigner. In fact, she was so angry she wouldn't talk to me for the rest of the day. All this may seem strange to you, but the point is that in Norwegian, the "day" of twenty-four hours is differentiated from the "day" meaning "daytime" (the two words being respectively, *døgn* and *dag*). Although my aunt actually used the English word "day" correctly in both senses, she somehow could not conceive that one word sufficed. It seems to me that the same thing is true for the feminist encountering the standard uses of the English word *man.* The thing that is insidious about this, is that if one were to be consistent, one should not only abolish generic *man* (by substituting *human being* or *person* or the like), but any similar

---

[6] I am indebted to Norberto H. G. Muller for initially pointing this out to me, and to Pei-Yi Wu and Bernard S. Solomon for their extensive comments. The most detailed account of this development available is given in Yuen Ren Chao, 1968, A Grammar of Spoken Chinese, Berkeley and Los Angeles: University of California Press, pp. 641-642.

sexist designations for animals, such as *dog* (generic *dog,* masculine *dog,* feminine *bitch*), *cat* (generic *cat,* masculine *tom,* feminine *cat* or, at least in some dialects, *queen*), *duck* (generic *duck,* masculine *drake,* feminine *duck*), etc. Of course, one might say that to carry things to such an extreme would be ridiculous, and that to quote a German saying "Nur Idioten sind konsequent" ("Only idiots are consistent"). But it strikes me that the original proposal to abolish generic *man* is idiotic in the absence of any evidence that it is truly harmful—and so I worry. Even the *day/night* business is not ideologically immune since as readers of Bachofen, the nineteenth century anthropologist, know, *night* was of central importance to matriarchal societies, but was supplanted by *day* when patriarchal societies overthrew the old order.[7]

Let me summarize a few of the things I have just said. In essence, they all reduce to the idea that words are arbitrary, and that sentiments follow social reality, not merely a change in labels. For example, consider words denoting professions once again. I think they are best compared with kinship terms, which, as Lewis Henry Morgan pointed out over a century ago, reflect but do not shape social situations. A society with clans is very likely to lump one's mother's sister along with one's mother under the same term since they both belong to the same clan, but to have a different term for one's father's sister who belongs to another clan. Clearly in this instance the linguistic structures come after the social fact and sometimes last after the social fact has changed. Although there would seem to be a straining towards consistency, the present is the output of the past and lags of various kinds often appear.

If it could be substantiated that "sexist" *he* or the like actually did produce reduced social expectations for women, it would be an exceedingly good case for the Whorfian hypothesis. Especially so because as far as I can see, this construction is a literary one that is hardly bound to make a profound impact on youth when it is forming its professional expectations. As a matter of fact, it is not unlikely that girls who are exposed to "sexist" *he*—that is, who come from professional and educated families with pretentions to correct grammar—would be the most likely to enter the professions to begin with. But all this is speculation. We have so little information relating rules of gender agreement with self image, and what we have is susceptible of a variety of interpretations. We do not even really know how *feminists* talk in unguarded moments. Future research along these lines is clearly needed. It is my general impression that many successful women simply ignore linguistic politics. One of these is my colleague Sydel Silverman. When she was elected chairman of our anthropology department, she was asked by the departmental secretary how she wanted to be referred to, as *chairman* or *chairperson.* Silverman replied that if she was going to be referred to as *chairperson,* she would feel obliged to changed her name to *Silverperson.* She did not change her name.

---

[7] See JOHANN JAKOB BACHOFEN, *Das Mutterrecht,* Krais. Stuttgart: Krais & Hoffmann.

A number of other studies dealing with gender marking in language have been pursued. Most of these can be summed up by the idea that gender assignments for inanimate nouns are not haphazard but somehow consistent. In a sense this view harps back to Protagoras who is said by Aristotle to have considered the question of gender in Ancient Greek. He is reported to have lamented the fact that *mênis* [μῆνις] "anger" and *péleks* [πῆληξ] "helmet" were feminine rather than masculine—presumably because he felt that they were more clearly associated with men than with women. In the same vein, Aristophanes ridicules Socrates in *The Clouds* for worrying about the word *alektruón* [ἀλεκτρυών] meaning somewhat anomalously both "rooster" *and* "hen" and for making up an unnecessary new word (never found in normal Greek) *alektrúaina* [ἀλεκτρύαινα] for *"hen"* by analogy of *léaina* [λέαινα] "lionness" to *léon* [λέων] "lion."[8]

Several theories about gender assignment have been proposed, some egregiously wrong. An early writer on the subject, James Harris, in 1751 maintained that the sun was a naturally masculine object and the moon naturally feminine—totally ignoring the reversed genders in Germanic and Russian. Two more recent studies are of some interest. One by Leigh Minturn (1965, A cross-cultural linguistic analysis of Freudian symbols, *Ethnology*), suggests that there is a consistent tendency to classify nouns denoting masculine symbols in the Freudian sense as masculine in gender, but that this is less obvious for feminine symbols. Ten languages were used in his sample: French, German, Russian, Greek, Irish, Maharata, Arabic, Tunic, Nama Hottentot, and Hausa. Unfortunately, most these are Indo-European. However, my own subjective and unsystematized review of gender assignment in Oceanic languages tends to support his contention, especially strikingly with the word for "spear" which for example in Anyula and a number of other Australian languages takes masculine agreements even though in linguistic form it should fall into a neuter class. But whether "spear" is masculine because it functions as a phallic symbol or because it represents the tool associated with men par excellence or because of some other reason is not obvious.

Robert and Ruth Monroe (1969, A cross-cultural study of sex gender and social structure, *Ethnology*) have tested the notion that a patri-biased society should have more masculine nouns in the associated language than another kind of society. Using virtually the same sample as Minturn,[9] they find that this does indeed tend to be so. Unfortunately, their corpus does not permit a comparable test for matri-biased societies.

Sir James George Frazer, familiar as the author of *The Golden Bough,* tried in 1900 to suggest an origin for grammatical gender in terms of the different linguistic behaviors of men and women that had been reported for various societies. Before examining Frazer's theory, let us consider the

---

  [8] These details, and some of the following, are given in R. H. ROBINS, 1972, *A Short History of Linguistics.* Indiana University Press. Bloomington & London.
  [9] Lebanese (Arabic), Kanawa (Hausa), Nama Hottentots, Gujarati, Irish, French Canadians, Byelorussians, Greeks, Dutch, Khasi.

kinds of differences that have been attested, in line with what Bodine has called sex-exclusive differentiation. The earliest record of such a difference is a report by J. B. du Tertre from 1654: *Histoire Generale des Isles d. S. Christople, de la Guadeloupe, de la Martinique et Autres dans l'Amerique* (Paris; Thorne and Henley say the publication date is 1664, quoting Jespersen 1922). Here he describes the difference of speech between the men and women among the Caribs. The general picture drawn by early writers on this subject was that of invading Carib speakers who conquer the Arawak, exterminating the men but intermarrying with the women. The Carib men and the Arawak women are said to have maintained their own languages. Subsequent scholars have doubted that two different languages were actually used or at least continued for long; Jespersen for one points out that from seventeenth-century materials only about one-tenth of the vocabulary of men and women really differed.

Be that as it may, occasionally great differences are found in the linguistic behavior of the two sexes, sometimes involving truly different languages. For example, in the last century in some part of Paraguay, the women were reported as being monolingual in Guaraní, the men bilingual in Guaraní and Spanish. The men always spoke Spanish among themselves (in honor of and in order to maintain the "race," as an early observer put it). For the present century, Joan Rubin found that almost the reverse is true: men whose first language was either Spanish or both Guarani and Spanish, tended "to use more Guarani with other men, but to use Spanish with women who are their intimates. Women, on the other hand, whose first language was either Spanish or both, tend to use Spanish to both male and female intimates" (1970:528).[10]

The earlier Paraguayan situation has recently been repeated (with suitable changes) among the Gimi of the New Guinea highlands. According to Gillian and David Gillison (personal communication), both men and women speak Gimi but only the men speak Pidgin English, which seems to be used virtually as a secret language to exclude women. It is not only that men have more contact with the outside world: young boys are deliberately taught Pidgin apparently as part of socialization into the men's world. Although this is an area of culturally instituted extreme sex antagonism centering on fear of menstrual pollution, the Gimi are not unique. My impression from the ethnographic literature is that men more frequently develop secret languages than women, e.g., in affiliation with puberty rites of passage. Walbiri Upside Down Talk reported from Central Australia by Kenneth Hale is a case in point. (For a convenient discussion of Upside Down Talk, see Robbins Burling, 1970, *Man's Many Voices'* Holt Rinehart and Winston, New York pp. 154-156.) If this observation is true, I suppose that it can readily be correlated with the fact that such rites are more general, communal, public, and spectacular for boys than for girls. And

---

[10] Bilingual usage in Paraguay, *In* Joshua A. Fishman, Ed., *Readings in the Sociology of Language*, The Hague: Mouton.

perhaps this correlation can in turn be correlated with the explanations offered by John Whiting and his associates, involving the need for same sex
identification of social roles—easier for girls brought up with their mothers
than for boys also brought up with their mothers. The thesis suggested by
Robin Lakoff that in the English-speaking world, boys and girls both learn
"women's language" (which boys eventually will have to change) makes
sense in this general context and probably applies in all societies—particularly strongly in those with mother-child households. Accounts of the
Carib situation mentioned above suggest that boys speak like their mothers
and do not use pure Carib "until they were of an age to associate with men,
when they discarded them [sic] non-Carib words as effeminate" (J. N. Rat,
1897, "The Carib language as now spoken in Dominican West Indies," *The
Journal of the Anthropological Institute of Great Britain and Ireland*,
27:293). There are some unanswered questions about this thesis of a very
practical kind, however. For example, in some societies such as that of the
traditional Sara of Ubangi, women wear huge lip plates or labrets making it
impossible for them to pronounce clearly, especially labial consonants. Accounts for these societies do not suggest that little children speak without
labials or in other ways copying the extraordinary speech of women, but
nothing definite has been recorded about this to my knowledge.

Some varieties of sex-exclusive differentiation can readily be explained
in terms of particular marriage rules such as local group exogamy. Thus, to
return again to the Gimi, the men of the village of Ubagubi have to marry
women from other areas, generally choosing women from the neighboring
villages of Kuasa and Gusaleve. Apparently a sound change had occurred in
Ubagubi but not elsewhere to the effect that an original /k/or /g /has
become /ʔ/. Hence, the men in this village will call it /ubaʔubi/ but the
women (who come from elsewhere), /ubagubi/. The systematic sex differentiation is in finer analysis merely geographical. Children up to the age
of about nine or ten speak inconsistently using either /k/ and /g/ or /ʔ/.
Girls eventually will move out to k/g speaking villages and adopt their
usage, but boys will remain and after ten consistently use /ʔ/.

Probably most of the genderlect differences found cannot readily be explained in terms of exogamy. These differences range from most features of
pronunciation to morphological distinctions, such as those found in
Japanese or in Chiquita, where men have a gender system overtly marked in
nouns and women lack it. The Japanese example is of interest because of its
great complexity: it intersects and overlaps with stylistic differences, on the
one hand, and language levels on the other, indicating various degrees of
deference and assertiveness between speakers. One Japanese woman several
years ago told me a story from her own life about how she modified her own
usage to accommodate a nontraditional situation. She had been made the
director of a certain department and had several men working under her.
The situation was linguistically intolerable from the traditional point of
view. For her to speak to her male subordinates in women's language would
have been equivalent to denying her own authority. She found the option of
adopting men's language as too gross even to be attempted. Her solution:

speak English. This solution was possible because all the men knew English themselves, and so in a sense English functioned as a kind of neutral intersex style level of Japanese, much as Indonesian is said sometimes to function as a neutral level in Javanese.

To return to Frazer's theory mentioned several pages ago. As I have said, he assumed that in some way there was a causal relationship between the existence of genderlects and the development of gender classes. His main theory is that what started out as morphological differences in genderlects eventually became reinterpreted to become genders. Thus, he argued, we could conceive of a language where men might say *equus* for "horse" but women, *equa* for the same notion. In such a language, the -*us* would mean "man speaking," the -*a,* "woman speaking." Through time, the value of the suffixes changed and -*us* would come to mean "male," the -*a,* "female"—referring now to the thing denoted by the noun rather than the speaker. The result: *equus* meaning "male horse"; *equa,* "female horse" or "mare." Although such an explanation cannot be ruled as impossible, and the Chiquita language is reported as having different gender systems in the two genderlects, it should be noted that no known language in the world today approaches Frazer's hypothetical stage. Reaction to this theory has been practically nil, but Arnold van Gennep at the beginning of the century had kind words for it.[11] Bodine has more recently called Frazer's 1900 paper "groundbreaking." But no one to my knowledge has compiled evidence to support his reconstruction, which is not particularly compelling to my mind.

One of the more fruitful areas of investigation and the last I shall discuss here deals with what Bodine calls sex preferential differences. These are differences that are statistically associated with one sex rather than the other but are not exclusively so. Thus, as Lakoff has pointed out, what she calls "women's language" in English is found not only among women, but also can be found among male hippies, homosexuals, and academics—men, she believes, who can be characterized in some sense as rejecting traditional masculine values. The distinctive features of "women's language" are: the avoidance of profanity and cursing, general conservatism and correctness, and the emphasis on indirectness and politeness—mechanisms that tend to isolate the speaker socially and to prevent the speaker from being taken seriously. To these mechanism we might also add the phenomena attendant upon interruption, to be discussed by Candace West later in this volume.

Lakoff's own work in this area is interesting for a number of reasons. Although she derives her approach from various aspects of the generative-transformational school of linguistics (notably the idea of *co-occurrence*), she practically re-invents the notion of *configuration* associated with the work of Ruth Benedict, Margaret Mead, and Gregory Bateson in the anthropological field of culture and personality. Both Lakoff and the an-

---

[11] As quoted by Tagliavini, *op. cit.,* p. 131 fn.

thropologists are concerned with ideal types or stereotypes that play up only a few of the possibilities within the spectrum of human potentials. For Lakeoff, this spectrum is seen as a continuum between the poles of clarity and camaraderie. A number of other linguistic investigations are relevant here, e.g., Basil Bernstein's nonrestricted and restrictive codes. Dell Hymes's attempted typology of speech styles could also be fit in. Although his article "Models of the interaction on language and social life"[12] does not especially deal with "genderlect" differences, he does indicate that dimensions such as verbose/laconic, voluble/taciturn can be different in a single speech community along sex lines. The one example he gives is the Araucanian type, where men are ideally voluble, good orators, and general conversationalists, whereas women are ideally quiet, speaking preferably in whispers.

For the most part, Lakoff seems to believe that women's language as found in English will probably be found in all language communities. Interestingly enough, with regard to the feature of linguistic conservatism she mentions as part of women's language, it was noted as a feminine trait as early as Plato in his dialogue *The Cratylus.* I have tried to find counterexamples in the ethnographic literature. Few accounts are full enough to be conclusive, but some are suggestive. Consider for example Elinor Keenan's study of a community on Madagascar, where women are said to go against the traditional linguistic norms.[13] Here it is the women, not the men, who are direct and brusque, and not concerned with the niceties of grammar. And it is they who are said to have the power in the society—though this is not clearly demonstrated.

Margaret Mead's work on the Tchambuli of New Guinea was especially consulted because she described them as a group in which Western notions of masculinity and femininity were reversed. Alas, very little information about speech styles appears in her book. The most extensive description she gives that is relevant for us is the following:

> . . . whereas the lives of the men are one mass of petty bickering, misunderstanding, reconciliation, avowals, disclaimers, and protestations accompanied by gifts, the lives of the women are singularly unclouded with personalities or with quarreling. For fifty quarrels among the men, there is hardly one among the women. Solid, preoccupied, powerful, with shaven unadorned heads, they sit in groups and laugh together.
>
> . . . Here again the solidarity of women, the unessentialness of men, is demonstrated. (*Sex and Temperament in Three Primitive Societies* 1935, p. 257).

[12] In JOHN J. GUMPERZ & DELL HYMES, 1972, *Directions in Sociolinguistics,* New York: Holt, Rinehart and Winston.

[13] "Norm-makers, norm-breakers: uses of speech by men and woman in a Malagasy community." in RICHARD BAUMAN & JOEL SHERZER, 1974, *Explorations in the Ethnography of Speaking,* London: Cambridge University Press.

Some forty years later, Deborah Gewertz doing field work among these same people (their name is now written as Chambri), noticed no essential style differences that reverse Western notions. It must be recalled, as Gewertz has pointed out to me, that when Mead visited them, there had been an upheaval in the traditional culture and that this period in their culture history could hardly be called normal (personal communication).

The two instances I have just mentioned just about exhaust the literature as far as counterexamples to Lakoff's thesis go. Futher cross-cultural studies are clearly needed.

Sexual linguistics raises a number of fundamental questions involving not only politics but also cognition, language acquisition, language typologies, reconstruction, and a great many other areas. The papers in the rest of the conference are contributions to answering these questions.

Abstract

LINGUISTIC MODELS AS POLITICAL SYMBOLS: GENDER AND THE GENERIC "HE" IN ENGLISH

EDWARD H. BENDIX

Is English a sexist language?

Since the author is an anthropological linguist, it is no wonder that this question generates the preliminary questions of what we mean by *English* and what we mean by *language,* to say nothing about what we mean by *mean.*

English is not a monolithic entity. As an abstraction it includes numerous dialects ranging from some that look more Danish to those that reflect African structures. As to Bendix's definition of language, the boundaries between linguistic and non-linguistic behaviors depend on which linguistic paradigm provides the model for a particular inquiry. The subject matter of this paper is precisely the multiplicity of descriptive models of language that are implied by various answers to the question of whether English is sexist or not.

In most linguistic paradigms, semantics is restricted to referential or denotative meanings. Bendix explores beyond referential significance to connotations, which entail belief and knowledge, and thus enters the field of communication. Even further from the traditional boundaries of linguistics, he pursues responses to pronouns in terms of inferences made from contextual cues found in situations in which utterances are made.

Bendix stresses that language theories mediate between the data and the social views held by diverse factions on the issue of language management or applied linguistics. Language is not only a means of communicating about affairs, as opposed to those affairs, but language is also symbolic of social relations.

Consider the following utterance illustrating Bendix's inquiry:

If anyone has a question, he/she should raise his/her hand.

Do the pronoun choices involved (including *their,* or using both *he or she* rather than either one of them) escape social biases? Whether they do or not, is the solution within the province of language or not? Bendix states: "To assert that English is sexist is to say that speakers are sexist when they do not make use of nonsexist options." On the other hand, what seems nonsexist to some is doubly sexist to others. The theory of language implicit in the political position taken, then, follows from that position and does not determine it.

Three theories concerning the meaning of the pronouns *he* are described by Bendix. The first maintains that *he* is semantically marked exclusively for the male sex, but that the feature "male" can be suspended when *he* occurs with in indefinite antecedent. According to the second theory, *he* is unmarked for sex or gender. Only context can determine whether the referent is male, female, or both. *She,* on the other hand, is marked for female sex. In the third theory, both *he* and *she* are treated as homonyms (or polysemes). One meaning refers to sex and the other to gender; the latter is arbitrary, thus allowing *he* to refer to both males and females.

Beyond these strictly linguistic theories, the pragmatics of the phenomena demonstrates that a neutral *he* may nevertheless connote maleness even when applied to females. Even in gender languages, connotations can actually clash and display leakage. The German *Mädchen,* "girl" is grammatically neuter and thus takes *es,* "it." But colloquially, the mandatory agreement is often dropped, and *sie,* "she" is substituted.

The final subject is a consideration of whether changing a generic *he* will change social behavior. When people already have beliefs/knowledge about the distribution of sex roles among statuses, language usage may only be a symptom and a reminder, as in such phrases as "the doctor . . . *he*," or "the secretary . . *she*." But when linguistic connotations function as the source and reinforcement of images, language can influence behavior, particularly among children in the enculturation process. Adults seem influenced not by language reform as a carrier of information, but as a political symbol in its own right.

Editors

LINGUISTIC MODELS AS POLITICAL SYMBOLS: GENDER AND THE GENERIC "HE" IN ENGLISH

Edward H. Bendix

Department of Anthropology, Hunter College, City University of New York
New York, New York 10021

Graduate Center, City University of New York
New York, New York 10036

In recent years a good deal of activity has focused on the generic use of the pronoun *he,* as well as on other aspects of English-speaking usage involving sex/gender distinctions.[1] It is clear that we have been witnessing a familiar concern with language as a symbol of social problems. Arguments have used linguistic data as evidence to prove (or deny) that the language manifests the sex-based biases of society. The evidence has been used for (or against) proposals to reform the language by replacing generic *he* with *he or she, he/she, s/he, they,* etc. Much less obvious, however, has been the fact that the positions depend crucially on implicit or explicit linguistic theories, that these various theories could indeed be seen as the true symbols used for the social contentions. Thus it is time to look at theories, making implicit ones explicit, in order to see how well they support the political ends to which they have been turned. For it is these theories which must mediate between the linguistic data and the political views asserted.

BACKGROUND

Any positions taken here, then, are at least intended to be about matters of method and theory and not about the issues themselves. The main argument, however, will not be clear unless we first digress into making several points of a background nature. These concern (a) the position of specialists as opposed to nonspecialists, (b) the truth of statements about meanings, (c) whether discriminatory attitudes involve referential meaning or inferred connotations, (d) the causal relations between symbols and their referents, (e) the relevance or irrelevance of etymology to the meanings of symbols, (f) what we refer to when using the term "the English language," and (g) what is meant by grammatical gender.

(a) If we wish to look at statements linking aspects of language with aspects of social relations, then assertions made by different specialists and nonspecialists must be viewed in the same light. Here we cannot take it as a given at the outset that the *a priori* linguistic or social assumptions of re-

[1] This is a revised and expanded version of a paper presented at the 73rd Annual Meeting of the American Anthropological Association, Mexico City, November 1974. Since it is a more general analysis of various views and does not cite much of the relevant research, the reader is referred to Thorne and Henley (1975:207-228) and Key (1972, 1975) for more detailed citation and discussion of the literature. I thank Mariam Slater and the anonymous reviewers for providing valuable perspective in the preparation of this final version.

0077-8923/79/0327-0023 $01.75/2 ©1979, NYAS

searchers are necessarily of a different order from those of other people.[2] The difference between actors and their investigators is simply a difference between actors. Also, by way of example, particular linguists may have a grasp of linguistic theory, but their theoretical concerns may have led them to data not directly relevant to their social or political assertions, whereas particular psychologists may be looking at relevant linguistic data but not have the grasp of linguistic theory necessary for converting them into arguments that are relevant. Individuals of either field may make unwarranted assumptions about the social representativeness of their data sources or of the situations in which the data were collected.

(b) Indeed, *all* statements about language involve underlying linguistic theories and sets of assumptions, each contributing in its own way to conclusions drawn from data (when data are used and of whatever value the data are). This epistemological stance is on even firmer ground here since the question of the generic *he* is at least in part a semantic one, and of all linguistic interests meaning is the most remote from direct observation. Anthropologists involved with ethnographic semantics in particular have faced the question of the reality or truth of theoretical statements about the meanings underlying verbal behavior (Wallace, 1965). Can there be a true description of the meanings of items found in language in contrast to which alternative descriptions of these items are only a playing around with constructs that may at best account for the same data? At the level of abstraction of semantic generalization, however, this God's truth/hocus-pocus distinction (Burling, 1964) is untenable (Tyler, 1969). Semantic statements should be evaluated, but never with the goal of finding the one true one.

(c) And if the question of the generic *he* is at least in part a semantic one, it is not clear how large a part. For example, the "generic" part may be separated out as a function in which pronouns are used but which is not part of the meaning of any of them, whether *he, she, he or she, they, you,* etc. (Martyna, 1978). Further, one approach to meaning could urge that discriminatory and negative attitudes said to be encoded in the generic *he* are better considered as connotations or their analog rather than as part of referential meaning. Another approach might not consider such attitudes as part of language at all. This depends on how some linguistic theory might define the term "language," and on how much of culture is consequently seen as falling within its scope. In any event, the communication of discriminatory attitudes would be handled best in a theory of communication, and not in a semantic theory of reference.

(d) Furthermore, besides being a *means* of communication about the affairs of culture, rather than those affairs themselves, language is also well known to be in various ways *symbolic* of social relations. We find the frequent view in sociolinguistic writing that these relations, and any changes in them, are likely to affect their symbolic expressions more than the other way around, as we should also expect that disputes about language are most

---

[2] For application of this principle to language-and-sex studies, see Kramer (1976).

likely to be disputes about something else. Language disputes, such as about sexist biases, are more likely to be settled when the social conflicts of which they are the expression are settled, although symbols may be one of the means for bringing about resolution of conflict. Thus, changing social awareness results in many people actually speaking in accordance with the belief that the pronoun *he* is always and only for reference to males. Older speech behavior uses this pronoun to have more general reference in certain contexts, which leaves it open to alternative linguistic analysis. Now that people have begun to modify their verbal behavior in this way, we have a language change in progress, one that is already being monitored by researchers (Bate, 1978).

(e) Historical knowledge of old meanings of words prior to their having undergone such change in times past is often used in arguments about their present meanings. This use of history can easily be irrelevant. For example, in the course of centuries of semantic change, the word *man* has substantially lost its relational sense of "husband." On the other hand, *wife,* has lost its sense "woman," keeping only its relational sense. We can, therefore, see why such a traditional formula as *I pronounce you man and wife* might now sound strange and be open to the interpretation that it expresses the social dependence imposed on a married woman. To say that *man* and *wife* changed their meaning is to say that the speakers changed their use. If *I pronounce you man and wife* is now seen as offensive by some people, or at best as inaccurate, then so it is for those speakers. To bring in history (i.e., the etymology) against this view is to bring another symbol into the dispute, history being one of the favorite bases for claims and counter-claims in human affairs.

But history is irrelevant to the current usage of those who see it differently. Symbols mean what their users make them mean and are successful if they convey the communicative intent. There may be differences of opinion and of usage, and here even authorities, national academies, and the like are only one group of interested people fighting it out with another. Humpty Dumpty was not all wrong in saying that when he used a word it meant just what he chose it to mean. He just failed to note that his hearers are equally free to interpret the meaning the word has for them. Of course, communication may suffer in the process when shared understanding of intended meaning is lacking.

(f) Maneuvers on the symbolic battlefield prompt us not only to investigate claims about the meanings of words in a language. The nature of the whole abstraction "Language X" would have to be considered, particularly as it is involved in evaluating the assertion that the English language is sexist. What sort of relevant abstraction does the label "English language," refer to? And what purpose is served in the present context by reifying it as the assertion does? Whatever we conclude on this level, on a less abstract level we know that patterns of some speech varieties included for various reasons under the umbrella of English remind us of descriptions of other languages. Some remind us of Danish, others, in their grammar and phonology, of West African languages. And there are historical reasons that can be given to account for such instances.[3] Language can be observed only in the behavior of individual people. What we have to deal with, then, in making judgments about what is usually called English, are alternative, overlapping representations, descriptions, or theories about this abstraction, devised or believed by many contributors to the field and ranging between the professional linguistic and the folk-linguistic. We are talking about linguistic descriptions said to be of English and see any specific statements about it as partially dependent on some particular linguistic theory and on the data used by the describer.[4]

(g) Since the term "gender" is used here in a technical, linguistic sense as well as others, a word should be said about it. Gender means a category, not a sex. It refers to the classification of nouns in a language when in that language such things as adjectives or pronouns are said to change their forms to agree or concord with nouns. That is, adjectives or prounouns show differential grammatical behavior with respect to different noun classes. If linguists must set up gender classes for nouns in a language to account for the differential behavior of other parts of speech than nouns, the language is then said to belong in the category of gender languages. Gender classes of nouns in a given language may or may not each have their respective themes, e.g. "female," "animate," "abstract," "portable." That is, in linguistic usage they need not have anything to do with sex—they do not, for example, in the Bantu languages—although in most of the familiar European languages they do. If a gender class consists mostly of nouns referring to inanimate (i.e., nonsexed) things but includes virtually all nouns for female beings, it will typically be called the feminine gender class of the language. Since most of the nouns refer to inanimates, we would call this a case of primarily arbitrary gender classification: the nouns for the most part do not share a common feature of sex nor any other discernible semantic theme. But where almost all the nouns in a given class in some language do refer to biologically female beings, as in English, we speak of natural gender. Although the nouns in such a natural gender class happen to share a common semantic theme, it is still a classification based on what is seen as grammatical agreement or concord behavior of nonnouns (see also below on concord violation and note 10).

---

[3] This is not to say that there is always general agreement about which umbrella, if any, a given "dialect" or other speech variety belongs under nor about how strong its credentials are for belonging there. The literature has numerous examples of disputed and shifting language identifications in other parts of the world (e.g., Gumperz, 1971a). In the U.S., linguists and nonlinguists alike have been at loggerheads about the degree to which a variety called by such names as "Black English Vernacular" is English or even exists. This issue was never independent of politics, neither for linguists nor for other Americans. Nor could it ever be simply a linguistic question, since one or another answer was too easily made into people's symbolization of the degree to which the segment of the U.S. population categorized as "Black" was American with right of equal access to social goods.

[4] We say "partially" since political goals and other biases can additionally affect the availability, perception, and selection of both data and theory (Gumperz, 1971b:218; Labov, 1971:159-165, 1972, 1973:112-114).

It is thus clear that we must distinguish masculine and feminine gender, as grammatical terms, from male and female sex, as biological and semantic terms. Gender languages may have occasional nouns that are by grammatical behavior, say, feminine gender but with a male as the typical referent, e.g. French *recrue* "recruit." It is in a nonlinguistic sense that "gender" is also used to refer to sex-related role assignments in a society.

PRONOUN CHOICE

Against this background, let us now take up the main topic, namely the third-person pronouns *he* and *she*. According to many descriptions they present the speaker with a forced choice for purposes of gender or sex reference. They have become a socially painful symbol and focus of interest of certain nonlinguistic concerns. The pronoun choice is seen on the basis of some implicit or explicit description as an expression and/or shaper of differential social attitudes and behavior toward males and females. Changing the usage, an action in applied linguistics, is believed to have beneficial social consequences. Although this language management is already having observable effects in the speech of individuals, it is not clear whether the changed pronoun usage is an expression, rather than a shaper, of changing cultural attitudes. For that matter, the new usage may, in some people's mouths, be an advertisement of adherence to the new social awareness which may or may not be borne out in substantive behavior. In many circles, it is by now difficult to follow the generic *he* usage without appearing to be making a contrary symbolic statement, and in fact many people so use it.

The problem as frequently stated is that we must choose between *he* and *she* even when referring to an indefinite person of unspecified sex. For example, we are forced to choose between *If anyone needs a pencil, he should ask for one* and *If anyone needs a pencil, she should ask for one.* Or, we choose between *someone* matched by the pronoun *he* and *someone* matched by *she*. *Anyone/someone* matched by *they* is also said to be available as a choice. The guardians of language are cited as requiring generic *he* in such cases. Likewise, for indefinite noun phrases, such as *a person, a doctor, a nurse, a poet, a secretary,* etc., the forced choice is between *a person* matched by *she* and *a person* matched by *he, a doctor . . . she/a doctor . . . he, a secretary . . . she/a secretary . . . he,* etc. One argument runs that the choice of *he* or *she* for such indefinite noun phrases is not an automatic, grammatically determined one as frequently claimed but reflects the speaker's (cultural) expectations of what the sex should be (Ervin-Tripp, 1976a:147). An example would be someone who says *a secretary . . . she* or *a doctor . . . he* although aware that there are male secretaries and female doctors.[5]

As far as nouns referring to social roles are concerned, this argument has the evidence on its side. But the indefinite pronouns and some nonrole nouns, such as *a person,* which is virtually pronominal, must be separated

---

[5] In English an indefinite noun phrase, such as *a secretary,* in itself is indeterminate as to whether or not a particular referent of the noun phrase is said to exist on any given occasion of

out for different treatment. Consider saying the following sentences to a mixed audience of males and females:

(1) -*he*: *If anyone has a question, he should raise his hand.*
(2) -*she*: *If anyone has a question, she should raise her hand.*

We can test whether (1) -*he* is (still) understood by most people as being addressed to all members of the audience and (2) -*she* understood as excluding the males in some way. (e. g., Martyna, 1978). We can also test for differential understanding of (1) -*he* vs. (2) -*she* when addressed to an all-female audience and to an all-male audience.

Let us say that the communicative intent of the speaker is that the message be understood as applicable to anyone in an audience. Then let us say that (2) -*she* would be communicatively successful only in the all-female audience whereas (1) -*he* would work for an all-female audience although now such a group might contain members who would still understand the communicative intent of the speaker but draw further conclusions, as might indeed some members of a mixed group, and possibly take corrective action. In any case, we would not have the kind of communicative breakdown that we could assume would occur if (2) -*she* were addressed to an all-male audience.[6]

---

use. For example, in "We have *a great secretary. She* can . . . ," the pronoun *she* is used because a particular female person is in fact meant. However, in "What you need is *a secretary. She* will . . . ," it cannot be inferred that the speaker has any particular person in mind so that the choice of *she* rather than *he* must be motivated by other than reference to a particular person. It is this latter type of *use* for nonspecific and generic reference that we are concerned with. The actual linguistic *form* of noun phrases can be definite or indefinite, singular or plural, for example *A secretary/The secretary is the mainstay of an office, Secretaries are the mainstay of an office, A secretary who . . . , Any secretary who . . . , Secretaries who . . . ,* etc.

[6] It should be stressed that the preceding, although reasonable, are only assumptions. For example, (1) -*he, If anyone has a question, he should raise his hand,* addressed to a *mixed* audience might leave some of the female members with vague or not so vague doubts about whether they can safely infer that the speaker intended them to be fully included although they would be less likely to feel that they were clearly meant to be excluded. Doubts can arise because contextual cues for making inferences are a matter of the individual's perception and thus subject to various background factors. This indeterminacy will be returned to later. It is, however, one that can be experienced by males under certain circumstances. For example, the writer's first three children were female. Reading Dr. Spock's well known child care book at that time left him with the vague feeling that the Doctor may not have been talking to him as a parent of daughters since the book followed the tradition of the field of using the pronoun *he* in referring to an unspecified child. Because there are generally believed to be differences of behavior between female and male children, it was not clear when descriptions of what "he" typically did at a given age also applied to girls.

On the other hand, (1) -*he* addressed to an *all-female* audience is not as likely to suffer from this indeterminacy since there are no males present to which *he* could preferentially refer. But another problem arises in this case. Although the social context is logically compatible only with the generic interpretation of *he,* the actual *use* or (1) -*he* addressed to an all-female audience may vary with the speaker's social-class background. Thus, certain kinds of schools for girls and women trained them for the linguistic marks of proper group membership and made a point of inculcating rigid standards of correct grammar, including generic *he* to any audience. One of the co-editors of this volume reports her Bryn Mawr College experience in the early 1940s that public announcements in the cafeteria using *they* as a generic singular pronoun were greeted by the audience of college women with a chorus of corrective *he*'s.

ALTERNATE THEORIES

Given the preceding assumptions, how could different views of language account for such results? How would they include the fact that *she* and *he* are also, or primarily, used for exclusive reference to a female and a male respectively when referring to a definite person of specified sex? What implicit theories may be found in the views that English is or is not sexist? We must ask such questions because it is only by means of linguistic theories that one can get from the raw data of language behavior to political assertions. Since there seems to be agreement that *she* is marked for female sex and/or for feminine gender (the latter including *she* for countries, ships, etc.), alternative treatments of the pronoun *he* will be the main focus.

Consider a theory concerned with referential meaning. Let us suppose it says that there is one pronoun *he* and that it is semantically marked only for "male" sex. Take (1) -*he, If anyone has a question, he should raise his hand.* When this sentence was addressed to a mixed or all-female audience, we assumed successful communication with potential reference to a female. Such a theory needs a special semantic rule which says, in effect, that the feature "male" may be suspended when *he* occurs in combination with an indefinite antecedent. We will call this type a version of the "sex-linked *he*" theory. This version could be seen as the underpinning for calling English sexist in the matter of pronouns on the grounds that *he* is basically "male" in meaning and, when including potential reference to females, reveals the attitude that women are derivative and secondary. That is, the semantic rule would be made a rather literal representation of the attitude that females are derivative. The corrective frequently offered, *she or he, he or she, he/she, s/he,* of course does not attempt to change what *he* and *she* mean under the theory since it assumes the correctness of the theory. It is intended to change usage, i.e. to get rid of the need for the special semantic rule.

A second version of the sex-linked *he* approach is without the special semantic rule and seems to have been the implicit version for claims that with an indefinite antecedent the use of *he* reveals that women are not really referred to at all. This version could also be seen behind claims, frequently considered pedantic, that the usage is simply incorrect and should be replaced by *he or she* for this reason.

In another type, the "sex-neutral *he*" theory, *he* is unmarked for sex (or unmarked for gender). That is, its meaning (= its definition under the theory) does not include the semantic feature "male." However, it does share such features as "human," "singular," "pronoun" with *she*. It thus stands in an opposition with *she,* which *is* marked for sex, namely "female." Since human beings are defined as coming in two sexes, and *she* is "female," speaker-hearers can be said to infer that *he* refers to a male unless the context is interpreted as opposing this inference. Strictly speaking, such things as speaker-hearer inferences and beliefs about the world are not properly part of the sex-neutral *he* theory (nor of the sex-linked *he*) but fall under some more encompassing theory of communication, to which we will return. Leaving *he* unmarked is a typical linguistic device which a descriptive account can use to indicate that *he* can refer to both males and females. The pronoun *they* is also not marked for sex (nor for "human"), but since it does not stand in an opposition to any other third-person plural pronoun, "female" or otherwise, it does not urge speaker-hearers to the interpretation of reference to males.

A version of the sex-neutral *he* theory says that *he* is unmarked for gender, rather than unmarked for sex, whereas *she* is marked as feminine gender. This would be a theory which uses both grammatical gender and semantic sex features. Nouns referring unambiguously to females are by a rule feminine gender and take *she* as their pronoun. Nouns referring to males, as well as nouns phrases, indefinite pronouns, etc. with unspecified or mixed sex reference, are left with the unmarked *he* as their pronoun.

The sex-neutral *he* theory is a type more likely to occur to people trained in linguistics, particularly in marking theory, as a representation of what the forms in question "mean." One example (McCawley, 1974), reacting to language reform guidelines for editorial staffs, speaks of the two-edged sword of the common-gender *he* (sex-neutral *he*) as "less sexist than is generally thought to be the case," the trouble lying with the tendency to use only one of its edges, i.e. to use *he* only where male sex is (culturally) expected although not necessary. As a counterproposal to the expression *he or she* (or *she or he*), it is submitted that *he* "loses its supposed sexual bias if it is used consistently," i.e. as the pronoun for all cases of unspecified sex, such as always saying *a kindergarten teacher . . . he, your spouse . . . he* (and presumably also *a nurse . . . he, a secretary . . . he,* etc.) and not only a *a doctor . . . he, an executive . . . he,* etc. To institute the usage *he or she,* it is claimed, is really more sexist. It does "as much to combat sexism as a sign saying 'Negroes admitted' would do to combat racism—it makes women a special category of beings that are left out of the picture unless extra words are added to bring them in explicitly." This last criticism holds only if the sex-neutral *he* theory is taken as a representation of reality. Under the sex-linked *he,* it can be claimed that women do need extra words in order to be brought in explicitly, on the grounds that they have indeed been left out of the picture.[7]

---

[7] It would be a mistake to conclude from the above example that the proponent of the counterproposal, McCawley, a linguist, is anti-feminist. Objection to the *he-or-she* class of language reforms is logically and in practice independent of attitudes to the women's movement since such objection itself can arise from various interests that language usage can be made to symbolize: not just sexist interests, but also social class, elite ethnic, or simple professional proprietary sentiments over linguistic matters. A mentality of with-us-or-against-us, taking *he or she* as a symbol, could easily and falsely interpret a person's attitude to the reforms as a clear indication of that person's position with respect to the movement. Linguists who are active in the movement can take a variety of positions on the *he-or-she* reform. For example, Lakoff (1973:74-75 = 1975:44-45) questions the feasibility of changing such an ingrained core element of language behavior. On the other hand, Bodine (1976:193) considers that the language reforms are not coming fast or soon enough but regrets that social scientists are lagging behind in investigating the functioning and interpretation of the generic masculine so that reform must proceed without much scientific guidance as to whether or how the generic masculine does operate to exclude women. However, a sizable portion of the population is offended by this use of *he,* and for those who believe that it does exclude women, we must say that the meaning that comes to be attached to a symbol is its own evidence.

USAGE AND THEORY

Proponents of both approaches may be concerned with problems of usage and interpretation of pronouns, but their theories are not. Being referential only, the latter deal directly with what words refer to, not with the users of the words. They cannot encompass these speakers and interpreters who mediate between words and things referred to, who in fact are faced with the task of creating reference. Instead, quite often, usage is measured against the theories and found wanting in one way or another. That is, discussion of usage, tested or intuited, can only take place informally outside of the framework of the theories. Such discussion is thus not subject to the structural controls imposed on it if it were to take place within the organization of a more comprehensive theory. Consequently, much valuable material often appears merely in the informal portion of a treatment of data only to be vitiated by questionable conclusions unchecked by methodological rigor.

The proposal in the cited example above, that *he* be generalized to all cases of unspecified sex, is already the typical usage in writings on child rearing. The frequent use by others of the pronoun *it* for *child* could be seen as a continuation of the Old English grammatical neuter gender of this noun. For *child* the pronoun conveniently allows a speaker to avoid specifying *she* or *he* where the sex is unknown. But *it* is now used almost exclusively for inanimates, leaving many people with some discomfort when applying it to a human being. Thus typical writers on child rearing have jumped from the frying pan of the depersonalizing *it* into the fire of criticism that they are really only bothering to write about male babies.

Besides the *he or she* class of replacements for generic *he,* it has been suggested that the colloquial use of *they* for indefinite singulars be returned to respectable status on the grounds that this practice has historical legitimacy (Bodine, 1975). Thus, *anyone . . . they* is common, *a person . . . they* might be difficult for some speakers, but, for example, *a doctor . . . they* would strike many as inadmissible. For such cases as the last, the suggestion is that indefinite singulars be avoided in favor of indefinite plurals: *doctors . . . they* is good English.[8] The ease with which these proposals fit into actual English usage would indicate that speakers are not always forced to make a paradigmatic choice between *he* and *she* to remain communicatively successful but have other options. However, the lower frequency in use of these options would indicate the need for a special motivation to increase the frequency.

---

[8] Creating an entirely new, sexless third-person singular pronoun, as so many other languages have even when their associated cultures can be perceived as oppressive of women, has also been proposed, but it would require general agreement on a form and a more radical change in core speech habits and has so far not caught on, whereas reforms using existing resources of the language are working. In fact, the use of the existing resources seems to be leading to a new pronoun in the speech of some people by the more familiar mechanisms of language change. Thus, the felt clumsiness of *he or she* leads to its being shortened to *he/she,* pronounced as "he, she," and now one can occasionally hear certain young people say it as one word "heshe".

The point, however, is that many proposals to replace *he* for unspecified sex are based on the claim that the sex-linked *he* theory represents reality at present. If these proposals are successful in changing the speech habits of speakers, the claim will be a self-fulfilling one. As a consequence, it would be difficult in the future for linguists concerned with theories of true reference to describe English with other than the sex-linked *he* since the pronoun *he* would only be left to refer to persons definitely or potentially specified in a context as male. A theory could then still decide to make one of the two pronouns *he* and *she* unmarked for sex/gender as in the sex-neutral *he* theory, but which one is chosen would have become an arbitrary decision. For present usage, however, leaving *he* unmarked can still be argued for as motivated since *she* must be marked for female/feminine.

HOMONYMY AND POLYSEMY

A third type of referential theory, which may be mentioned for the record and passed over quickly since it does not seem to have figured much in the debate, uses homonymy or polysemy. For the version with homonymy, there are two pronouns pronounced (or written) *she* and two pronounced (or written) *he*. One *she* and one *he* are marked "female" and "male" sex respectively. The other *she* is not marked for "female" but for grammatically feminine gender, and the other *he,* for grammatically masculine gender. *Country, ship,* etc. are then marked as English nouns that allow a feminine *gender* assignment since they do not refer to things that possess sex. This marking would have to be treated as variable because usage of *she* for countries, ships, machines, etc. is variable and the pronoun *it* is also used. It is the inclusion of both biological or semantic sex marking and arbitrary gender marking in this theory that permits indefinite pronouns such as *anyone* to be marked for masculine gender, which, being arbitrary rather than biological, allows reference to females and takes the *gender* pronoun *he*. *Cat* and *dog,* for example, with typical pronominal reference *she* and *he* respectively even though known to come in two sexes each, could be considered as retaining Old English genders in part and marked as frequently being feminine and masculine gender respectively. These two nouns would thus take the gender *she* and *he* in such usage. In contrast to this homonymy version of the theory, the version with polysemy would differ merely in that there would be only one pronoun *she* and one *he,* and each would have two submeanings, a sex submeaning and a gender submeaning.[9]

---

[9] Our theme of the symbolic uses of theories could be pursued further into the heart of technical linguistics, for those who are interested in following. Science is embedded in society, and the problem of sexist biases has been felt in marking theory. Thus, we have so far discussed descriptive approaches using the features "male" and "female" along the two-valued dimension "sex." For greater economy, linguistic theories also use plus-and-minus notation. Instead of "male" and "female," we then typically find "plus male" and "minus male", i.e. [+ male] and [− male]. Depending on the language being described, the features [− female] and [+ female] respectively would be just as serviceable or might even be preferable given certain facts in the particular language. Since the grammatical/semantic dimension in question is ordinarily defined as having only two values, using [− male] is adequate for the purely linguistic purposes of syntax or accurate reference to females . . . adequate, that is, for a computer. But

CONNOTATION AND COMMUNICATION

Apart from any incorporation of grammatical gender, the theories discussed above have been theories only of true reference, as the term is used in philosophy. That is, they have been concerned with defining *he* and *she* in such a way that the definitions accurately reflect how these pronouns (are believed to be used to) *refer* to males and females. But purely referential semantics cannot be made to do the work of theories of communication. Broader approaches to semantics and communication in general would include more data to be accounted for, connotation, for example.

Connotation, or its analog in various psychological theories, can be included in or excluded from the class of data for which a given linguistic semantic theory holds itself accountable. It can be considered part of meaning or not. It goes beyond true reference since a word in any instance of use can still refer properly to a thing whether or not the word's connotations are considered accurate in that instance. For example, the pronoun *he* could be said to have the connotation "male" but not be strictly defined as "male." It could then be used for potential reference to an unspecified female. Likewise, a theory of oppositions, of which the sex-neutral *he* is an example, could say that the pronoun *he* stands in an opposition with *she,* which is marked "female." As with connotation, hearers can then be said to be ready to infer that *he* refers to a male unless a given context is interpreted as not allowing this inference. However, hearers' inferences and judgments of contexts go beyond considerations of reference or even semantics, and a theory of oppositions that does not go beyond reference such as the sex-neutral *he,* cannot properly deal with them. It is such things as connotations, inferences, judgments, and beliefs that we must look at to see why the generic use of *he* so easily lends itself to symbolization of sexism.

---

linguists are people, and the word "male" is not just a technical term of linguistics. [+male] and [−male] may come more easily to a male linguist. Also, such a use could hardly go unnoticed and was taken as a symbol or symptom of discriminatory attitudes. Why not [+female] and [−female] as the two values of the dimension? More importantly, by going beyond being a linguistic notational device, [−male] became a symbol of defining women by the absence of male characteristics; the minus itself acquired definitional meaning. Since females and males are to be defined independently by their respective characteristics, some linguists changed their notational features from [+male] and [−male] to [+male] and [+female]. That is, out of sensitivity to social inequities (or out of fright), they changed their linguistic theories from having one dimension or binary feature [±male], which is more economical, to having in effect two. Of course, economy is not the only consideration: whether the obvious nonlinguistic relation between the concepts of male and female should be made a linguistic one in the first place can be debated.

Other linguists have consistently used such independent features as [+female] and [+male] or [+feminine] and [+masculine] and although there obviously is a connection between the two members of a pair, have not formalized the connection as a linguistic dimension. Rothstein (1973:462) found himself obliged by the data of present-day Russian to use all four features just mentioned as binary features, a total of eight features. This is related, in part, to the continued use of many Russian masculine-gender role terms with increasingly frequent reference to women as women have moved into the roles, so that adjectives might agree either with the gender of the noun or the sex of the referent. Key (1972:20-22) evaluates some of the literature involving sex/gender in linguistic feature notation and should be consulted for a deeper discussion than this note gives.

It is becoming clear from an increasing number of tests of speakers that *he,* not unexpectedly, makes them think of "male" in a variety of contexts. If nothing else, one might expect this from the virtually exclusive use of a pronoun pronounced (or written) *he* for persons definitely specified as male. Any other pronominal usage, such as the generic, that is also pronounced (or written) *he* can thus also become associated with "male"—a phenomenon called stimulus generalization in certain psychological approaches. We can see the same phenomenon in European languages with largely arbitrary gender. In the terms of a gender model of grammar, speakers of such languages, in their strict usage, characteristically make the equivalents of the pronouns *he* and *she* (and *it*) agree or concord with the gender of nouns, whether animate or inanimate. Typically, also, nouns for persons of the same sex fall in the same gender class, thus giving the class, and its pronoun, that potential sex connotation in addition to gender. In the exceptional cases where connotation clash there may be leakage. Thus, in strict usage, German *Mädchen* "girl," neuter gender for historical reasons, takes the neuter pronoun *es* "it," but the colloquial tendency is to use the feminine gender pronoun *sie* "she."[10] Such languages are also used for literature, such as poetry, and fairy tales, that makes persons out of inanimate things. Unless such personification is given the sex that corresponds to the gender of the noun for the inanimate thing, the imagery fails, although neuter nouns allow some flexibility. Translation of this literature between languages is a frequently mentioned difficulty when one language assigns feminine gender to its noun for the inanimate and the other assigns masculine gender. This and other evidence from various languages shows that even with largely arbitrary gender there can be a latent association which is easily activated. For more detailed discussion of evidence (see Ervin, 1962).

Thus, no matter what weight a given theory attaches to one or another connotation, we are faced with the likelihood of having to treat "male" as latent in *all* usages of *he* that are not actually overt reference to a specified male individual. We can see whether this latency can be operationalized and by testing be found in speakers even when they are not actually aware of it. Some speakers may deny such a latency in their own intuitions of their language or deny that it can have any effect on their attitudes toward women. They will never, however, be the same once they have come into contact with proponents of the theory that *he* is always "male," call it part

---

[10] In addition to the more familiar European cases of "violation" of gender concord, instances of semantic precedence over gender classes from nonsex-based gender languages are found in Navaho (Landar, 1965) and Ojibwa (Black, 1969). The leakage has become a torrent in post-revolutionary Russian (Rothstein, 1973). From the semantic approach of form-content analysis, the concept of gender and the distinction between concord and concord violation in Spanish can be dispensed with and the apparent vagaries of the language unified into a single, coherent account (Otheguy, 1977). Ervin-Tripp (1976a:153) finds that what various kinds of psychological and linguistic evidence suggest is that gender is a property of a semantic concept rather than of a word, i.e. is best treated in a theory as part of meaning rather than of grammar.

of a process of brain-washing, consciousness raising, or simply the soften-
ing up that is the first step to a possible language change. Since language is
symbolic in various ways, to assert that English is sexist is to say that
speakers are sexist when, for whatever reasons, social, inertia, etc., they do
not make use of the options of a nonsexist connotation that perceived patterns of usage leave open to them. The "language" is simply one or another
description of patterns of speech and patterns of judgments about speech of
a segment of speakers.

But if one accepts the pronoun *he* as ever ready to connote "male," how
does one account for the correct inference that *he* is meant to include
females on given occasions of its use? To do so, we would need theories
more comprehensive than simply an inclusion of connotation: they would
have to encompass contexts, beliefs, and speaker-hearer inferences. By way
of brief example, let us return to nouns involving social roles and imagine
the kind of unusual test sentence that can force this whole inference process
closer to the surface, such as an occurrence of *a secretary . . . he,* as opposed to *a secretary . . . she.* We assume that the belief or knowledge is shared
by adult speaker-hearers that some secretaries are male, although a minority. Part of the process involves a hearer's perception or reconstruction of
background context including any knowledge of current sexual politics with
respect to language matters. Then *a secretary . . . he,* if it does not simply
lead to confusion, can be inferred to refer only to the minority of male
secretaries, although it would require a moment's reflection to arrive at this
inference, or it can be inferred to include all secretaries but also to be an indirect political statement by the speaker, and other possibilities. That is, we
would expect it to have a different impact from *a secretary . . . she,* with
which we might not evoke much of the inference process. Note that the
problem is not a violation of true reference since the pronoun *he* is not being
used to refer to a particular person of specified female sex. A linguistic
theory that uses connotations, in addition to referential meaning, could in-
corporate the cultural expectation that a secretary is likely to be female, re-
label it as the connotation "female" of the noun *secretary,* and then say
that this connotation and the connotation "male" of *he* clash. Unless the
theory goes beyond connotations, it still could not account for what
speaker-hearers do with this clash.[11]

---

[11] Since perception of context and other factors of the moment as input into the inference
process are so variable, the same person can draw opposite inferences from different tokens of
the same utterance type at different times. A theory of reference only, belonging to the second
version of the sex-linked *he* theory, could underlie the flat assertion that (1) -*he, If anyone has
a question, he should raise his hand,* addressed to a mixed audience simply excludes the female
members. A broader theory which makes room for the various features of context and other
inputs could get closer to accounting for a female member's inferring that the speaker of (1) -*he*
intended to include her and other females while she was participating *in vivo* but inferring that
she is excluded when asked to give a judgment about (1) -*he* in the context of a test for built-in
biases of the language. This difference in inference is especially possible if the social context of
testing involves the utterance in isolation rather than a token of the utterance in use and should
be a warning about test design as a factor in the kind of data obtained (McConnell-Ginet,

Conclusion

As long as speaker-hearers already have beliefs/knowledge of the sex distributions of, for example, secretaries, poets, firefighters, executives, language usage is only a symptom, symbol, and reminder of perceived social imbalances to be redressed by social means. The linguistic harm comes in directly when connotations or their analog function as the *source* (and reinforcement) of beliefs/knowledge about sex-role distributions, in the absence of contextual clarification e.g., the connotation "male" of *he*. As one anthropology student put it, she acquired the false information that all shamans are male from a label in a museum display with the usage *a shaman . . . he*. More importantly, we can expect similar processes in the enculturation of children, where images of potential future roles and the like are formed. Much attention has recently been directed to developing broader theories that include considerations of perception of context, beliefs/knowledge, and strategies of inference about the speaker's intended message, but these are still in a fluid state and go beyond the scope of this discussion.[12]

A question that needs further study is the effectiveness with which language reform can play any role in social change and the relation between linguistic symbols and social behavior in general.

Thus, for example, verbal behavior is said to be one expression of social attitudes but it is not always clear what we mean by "attitudes" (Wicker, 1969). They may be defined in terms of people's verbalizations, in terms of the results of indirect verbal tests, or in terms of people's actually observed behavior. The last would seem to be the most important socially.

In the same vein, will success in changing people's generic *he,* usage change their social behavior? Some types, skilled in the exercise of power, know how to manipulate symbols. They can promote employees to higher job titles without raise in pay or change from *chairman* to *chairperson* as

---

1976:189; Ervin Tripp, 1976b:10).

Similar tests for sexual biases in English in different parts of the U.S. have come up with conflicting results, and one wants to know what was not controlled for. Not just considerations of context, but control for subcultural differences by age, social class, region, and ethnicity are part of a good research design for sexual attitudes and their contribution to perception of context. Researchers must also avoid basing design on the myth of homogeneity of all Americans who are not obviously "ethnic" or "racial," a myth arising from the need for integration of diverse populations and served by the surface uniformity of American public culture. We must thus go beyond simply testing for American attitudes as though we were a homogeneous population and any convenient group of college students will do as a representative sample. We must also check whether our findings in fact correlate with or, because of unsuspected sampling biases, are skewed by stable residual ethnicity, the differing private cultures maintained and handed down through generations of American-born of ultimately diverse national origins and including different attitudes about sex roles (Glazer and Moynihan, 1963, 1970; Nahirny and Fishman, 1965; Fishman and Nahirny, 1966). In general, there are a number of potentially significant variables that turning to specialists in allied fields could reveal.

[12] For example, an approach that analyzes language purely as a means of communication and considers reference an activity performed by speaker-hearers as part of the inferential process can go about defining *he* and *she* quite differently since concern with reference has been shifted out of semantics.

long as the referent remains male. Clumsier types reserve *chairperson* for reference to women. Both can modify their generic *he* usage to something considered less sexist with no intention of otherwise changing their policies. Other people, as well, can make their changed pronoun usage express only their social enlightenment, accompanied perhaps by a change in verbalized attitudes, but keep their old behavior. These, however, have been misled into believing that the symbolic change *is* the social change and never notice the inconsistency with behavior. Nor might they want to notice the inconsistency, since behavior does not exist in a vacuum but is subject to other social forces too strong to be so easily overcome by mere manipulation of symbols. So, even if only consciousness raising was the intended goal, language reform misapplied may end up as no more than language change. Symbolic victories can be empty ones and, worse, be mistaken for real ones.

What has been missed is that the relation of a language symbol to what it stands for—here the social behavior—is arbitrary. The relation can be broken, the symbol replaced by another or given a new meaning. There is a tenuous chain of intimate interconnections that leads from our interests and experiences of social forces on to our social perceptions and thought and then finally to the symbolic expression. Action for social change that pulls on only one end of the chain and leaves the other anchored down can break a link.

Although there may be bidirectionality of influence along the chain, we must say, however, with what evidence we have, that the major influence travels from the social experience through the perception to the symbolic end. Social change must be effected primarily by political means with symbolic change only a salient, integral accompaniment. To increase the reverse flow of influence and start with language reform may be more effective with children, whose social perceptions are still forming and whose experience is narrow. With adults, however, language reform alone may not be enough. We have in fact been dealing with two symbolic aspects of language. One is language as a system of symbols for communicating information, which is what language reform, strictly speaking, affects. The other is language as a sociopolitical symbol in its own right. With adults, it may be the latter aspect, the broader social significance that comes to be attached to the details of a language reform, that must be emphasized if the symbolic is to play an effective part in the total effort at social reform.

The main theme of this paper has been the evaluation of linguistic theories for their relative strength in serving as such political symbols. It is perhaps in the nature of the symbolic human animal that this role is inevitable for language. If a theory says that the so-called generic *he* in fact excludes females, then it cannot account for the counter-evidence that people can correctly infer the intended inclusion of females. If experiments show that people's first association to the pronoun *he* is always "male," then this fact can be used as evidence against the common-gender or sex-neutral *he* theory. Neither theory could account for evidence that people can correctly understand "she" as included in generic *he* but that the inferential process for arriving at this understanding may be much more difficult and tenuous than inferring "he" from *he*. A more comprehensive theory of communication could. The point is that, if linguistic theories and descriptions of a portion of a language are to be used as political symbols, then those that successfully account for the largest spread of accurate, relevant observations can most successfully stand up to linguistic counterattack and thereby make the strongest symbols.

REFERENCES

BATE, B. 1978. Nonsexist language use in transition. Journal of Communication **28**:139-149.
BLACK, M. B. 1969. A note on gender in eliciting Ojibwa semantic structures. Anthropological Linguistics **11**:177-186.
BODINE, A. 1975. Androcentrism in prescriptive grammar: singular 'they', sex-indefinite 'he', and 'he or she.' Language in Society **4**:129-146.
— 1976. Investigating the generic masculine. *In* Dubois and Crouch, pp. 191-194.
BURLING, R. 1964. Cognition and componential analysis: God's truth or hocus-pocus? American Anthropologist **66**:20-28.
DUBOIS, B. L. & I. CROUCH, Eds. 1976. The sociology of the languages of American women. Linguistics. Trinity University. San Antonio, Texas.
ERVIN, S. M. 1962. The connotations of gender. Word **18**:248-261.
ERVIN-TRIPP, S. M. 1976a. Speech acts and social learning. *In* Meaning in Anthropology. Basso, K. H. & H. A. Selby, Eds. University of New Mexico Press, Albuquerque. pp. 123-153.
— 1976b. What do women sociolinguists want? *In* Dubois and Crouch, pp. 3-16.
FISHMAN, J. & V. C. NAHIRNY. 1966. The ethnic group school in the United States. *In* Language Loyalty in the United States. J. A. Fishman *et al.*, Eds. Mouton. The Hague. Chapter 60.
GLAZER, N. & D. P. MOYNIHAN. 1963, 1970. Beyond the Melting Pot. MIT and Harvard University Press. Cambridge, Mass.
GUMPERZ, J. J. 1971a [1957]. Some remarks on regional and social language differences in India. *In* Language in Social Groups: Essays by John J. Gumperz. Stanford University Press. Stanford, Ca. pp. 1-11.
— 1971b [1964]. Hindi-Punjabi code-switching in Delhi. *In* Language in Social Groups: Essays by John J. Gumperz. Stanford University Press. Stanford, Ca. pp. 205-219.
KEY, M. R. 1972. Linguistic behavior of male and female. Linguistics **88**:15-31.
— 1975. Male/Female Language. Scarecrow Press. Metuchen, N.J.
KRAMER, C. 1976. The problem of orientation in sex/language research. *In* Dubois and Crouch, pp. 17-29.
LABOV, W. 1971. The study of language in its social context. *In* Advances in the Sociology of Language. J. A. Fishman, Ed. Vol. I. Mouton. The Hague. pp. 152-216.
— 1972. Some principles of linguistic methodology. Language in Society **1**:97-120.
— 1973. The linguistic consequences of being a lame. Language in Society **2**:81-115.

LAKOFF, R. 1973. Language and woman's place. Language in Society 2:45-79.
— 1975. Language and Woman's Place. Harper and Row. New York.

LANDAR, H. 1965. Class co-occurrence in Navaho gender. International Journal of American Linguistics 31:326-331.

MARTYNA, W. 1978. What does 'he' mean?: use of the generic masculine. Journal of Communication 28:131-138.

McCAWLEY, J. D. 1974. [Letter to the Editor.] The New York Times Magazine, Nov. 10, 1974, p. 103.

McCONNELL-GINET, S. 1976. Intonation. In Dubois and Crouch, pp. 187-190.

NAHIRNY, V. C. & J. A. FISHMAN. 1965. American immigrant groups: ethnic identification and the problem of generations. Sociological Review 13:311-326.

OTHEGUY, R. 1977. A semantic analysis of Spanish EL, LA, and LO. Unpublished Ph.D. dissertation. Linguistics Program, Graduate School, City University of New York.

ROTHSTEIN, R. A. 1973. Sex, gender, and the October Revolution. In A Festschrift for Morris Halle. S. R. Anderson & P. Kiparsky, Eds. Holt, Rinehart and Winston. New York. pp. 460-466.

THORNE, B. & N. HENLEY, Eds. 1975. Language and Sex: Difference and Dominance. Newbury House. Rowley, Mass.

TYLER, S. A. 1969. The myth of P: epistemology and formal analysis. American Anthropologist 71:71-79.

WALLACE, A. F. C. 1965. The problem of the psychological validity of componential analyses. In Formal Semantic Analysis. E. A. Hammel, Ed. American Anthropologist 67(5) part 2:229-248.

WICKER, A. W. 1969. Attitudes versus actions: the relationship of verbal and overt behavioral responses to attitude objects. Journal of Social Issues 25(4):41-78.

Abstract

SEX, ROLE, AND SEX ROLE

JOHN BEATTY

In general anthropology there has been a renaissance in studying the interface between culture and biology. The relation has often been misconstrued, and it is easy to fall into a biological reductionism, a flaw in the older studies of race and behavior. Beatty suggests that we look into the nonreductionistic relation between an individual's reproductive organs—his or her "sex"—and the social role, or position in society that this individual plays. The third conceptual unit to be considered is the person's "sex role"—his or her performance in expressing sexual desire and/or satisfaction through sexual intercourse or other kinds of sexual interaction.

Beatty explores some interrelationships among the biological status of male/female, the social roles defined culturally as masculine/feminine, the influence of "sex roles," and the linguistic expression of these variable linkages.

The Western relation between sex role and social role is not universal. Beatty cites a number of cross-cultural variations. For example, among the Hong Kong Chinese and among the Japanese, masculinity is defined by the strength of the bonding between males, whereas virility is confined solely to the way a man manages his sexuality with women. Among English-speakers, masculinity is identified with virility. By contrast, no congruent concept characterizes a woman's "sex role" or actual sexuality. Moreover, this *fact* is reflected by an obligatory linguistic gap.

In American culture, behavior during the sex act is an aspect of role. Men are supposed to be aggressors, and women passive. These aspects of sex role and social role are reflected in attitudes toward male homosexuality. Among certain groups (including prisoners and some male prostitutes), men who have sex with other males are not regarded as homosexuals unless they play a passive role. Thus, a homosexual may be defined by the mode of behavior exhibited during the sex act rather than by reproductive identity. That is, his social role is merged with his sex role rather than being determined by his biological sexual identity.

Another language and culture considered is Mohawk, a branch of Iroquois. Here an interesting comparison is provided with Bendix's analysis of pronouns and Gregersen's observations on Mohawk pronouns in matrilineal society. For example, the third person singular makes three differentiations: masculine, neuter-zoic, and feminine indefinite. The feminine indefinite is used for women who are excluded from the speaker's category on the basis of being un-marriageable because of age or kinship. This grammatical form can also mean "one." The neuter-zoic is used with animals and inanimate nouns as well as with women who are potential mates, namely, adults of child-bearing age who are not close kin.

Linguistic and cultural attitudes toward Mohawk women, heterosexual and homosexual, coincide. They contrast with the cultural and linguistic attitudes to homosexual men.

Editors

SEX, ROLE, AND SEX ROLE

John Beatty

Department of Anthropology
Brooklyn College, City University of New York
Brooklyn, New York 11210

The relationship between biology and culture is a complex one that has puzzled anthropologists for years. Even as Boas and his students were trying to destroy the myths that bound race, language, and culture together, forces were at work that would cause the problem to raise its head again.

As anthropology had shifted away from the universalist approach put forth by the early cultural evolutionists and moved toward a new position of cultural relativism in the past, so today once again the pendulum swings back, and once again anthropologists (among others) have begun the return to cultural, linguistic, and psychological universals. They have proceeded to try to link these patterns to biological bases. As Chomsky linked his deep structure to a genetic structure, the ethologists place programs for behavior into the genes. Warfare is aggression; aggression is genetic; hence war is in our genes. As Lorenz (1963) and Ardrey (1966) gave us the biological basis for war, Fox and Tiger gave us the biological basis of political systems (1969).

Similarly, Jensen and others have returned to the biological determinism theories of psychology and re-opened the whole field of the relationship between genes, race, and I.Q., a relationship that most anthropologists thought had been laid to rest by the middle of the 1940s.

Recently, with the development of the women's movement, the biological issue had once again been reactivated by discussions of the foundations of sex roles. Sex roles are not unlike race in that both are involved with the linkage of some behaviors to some biological characteristics. Some people tend to feel that since the category is based on a biological characteristic, it is somehow "more real" than arbitrary, cultural categories, such as "beliefs." As a result, racial groups seem to have a more substantial reality about them than do those of "democrat" or "republican." In part, this may be related to the fact that one can alter one's own "cultural category" volitionally, but one needs to cause society to alter its classification system in order to change one's biological position in it. Often, cultural categories create the biological divisions, as when "social" race distinguishes certain groups, such as the Indios and Mestizos of Mexico, when physically, the groups are equally interbred.

This short digression is meant to make the point that cultural categories are just as cultural when they apply to biological divisions as when they apply to "belief" criteria.

This is clearly vital to the problems of sex, role, and sex role. Sex is a classification based on biological criteria. A person is male if he has male

43

0077-8923/79/0327-0043 $01.75/2 ©1979, NYAS

sex organs. A person is female if she has female sex organs. (Hermaphrodites, of course require a special term since they possess both sex organs. And it has been recently discovered that genetic and hormonal sex do not necessarily coincide.)

Role, on the other hand, is often defined as a set of behaviors identified with a given status. But what then are sex roles? Are they behaviors identified or caused by biological sex (i.e. because a person is male or female, he or she will exhibit specific behavior)? Or are they behaviors identified with a social status, e.g., "woman" or "man?" A third possibility is that sex role refers to the behaviors that occur during the sex act. This latter can clearly be related to "general" sex role as being the set of behaviors expected of a man or woman when they are having sex. These behaviors are clearly culturally variable. It is the relationship among these categories that I wish to examine here.

First, let us establish some basic terms to deal with the problem. On the whole, people may be biologically classified into two groups: males and females. Further, there are two statuses associated with these biological divisions: men and women. I will refer to the male image or role as "masculinity" and the female image or role as "femininity" while keeping in mind that each culture will have a different interpretation of these roles, value them differently and, so on. Last, I shall need two terms to refer to the sexuality of each. Male sexuality is "virility," but English does not have a term for the sexuality of women.

Status	Biology	Role	Sexuality
man	male	masculinity	virility
woman	female	femininity	?

Western society in general has tended to confuse the last two categories. Virility (i.e., a man's ability to perform sexually with a female) is for much of the West a large part of man's masculinity. Perhaps because women are not supposed to be involved with sexuality in Western morality, the missing term is not so surprising. It is, in traditional fact, almost an obligatory gap. The very concept which it would identify would be exactly that which would inhibit women from being feminine.

In English, in fact, one of the differences between "lady" and "woman" may be the sexuality linked with the term "woman." It is possible to construct sentences in English that make just such a distinction between the two terms. Speakers tend to reject "She's a masculine lady," but not "She's a masculine woman." When queried about one of the "sex goddesses," some native English-speaking males indicated the sexual quality in "She's *some* woman." When I persisted and said "X (the sex goddess) is a lady," I was corrected with a variant of the old joke: "She's no lady, she's a woman!" There is some ambivalence on this point among some, since "lady" is a subdivision of "woman" while at other times "lady" is directly opposed to "woman." A similar situation occurs with "man."

man		
man	woman	
	woman	lady

The confusion in the United States between the categories which have herein been labeled as "sexuality" and "role" is not found universally. It would appear from some work with Hong Kong Chinese and with Japanese that the two aspects, "sexuality" and "'role," are kept quite separate and have little if anything to do with each other. In American culture, it is difficult to imagine a recently married man sending his wife home to her mother so that an unmarried male friend could stay at his apartment with him and not have to go to a hotel. But this can and does happen in Hong Kong with no implications of sex.

It would appear that both the Japanese and the Chinese (among others) define masculinity by the strength of the bonding between males (i.e. by how well a man can maintain social relationships with other men), while virility is measured by how well he manages his sex behavior with women. Hence, it is possible for a man's virility to be questionable, but his masculinity may be quite secure (or vice versa). This separation of sex and role has important cross-cultural ramifications.

A Japanese male homosexual may be considered masculine if he maintains a good and appropriate life style, that is to say, if he maintains the proper social relationships with men publicly. If two Japanese married couples visit, it is not surprising for the men to sleep together in one room, while their wives share a different room. Nor would a Japanese find it odd that a married man would chose to sleep in the same room with a visiting male friend while his wife slept alone in another room. Most Americans find this hard to conceive of and suggest that they would be suspicious of the two men involved, and what their sexual relation was to each other.

This is not to say that Japanese give full approval to homosexuality. Quite the contrary. Japanese are upset about exclusive homosexuals, but it appears that the tension is caused by the feeling that homosexuals may be lonely in their later lives and will not have children to look after them. Beyond that, no one seems terribly concerned, and Japanese seem to regard homosexuality as an irrelevant part of social relationships. They are puzzled that anyone would stop being friends with someone because they had learned of a friend's homosexuality. American homosexuals have indicated some surprise that some of their heterosexual friends were willing to remain friends with them after their homosexuality became known.

Although it would be interesting to see if Japanese homosexuals "come out of the closet," most Japanese interviewed indicated some difficulty in understanding the question. It was not clear why anyone would want to make an announcement of one's sexuality, since sexuality (homo or hetero) is private and hence irrelevant to anyone else except in the context of the sex act.

The fact that Americans tend to terminate friendships with, and otherwise discriminate against, homosexuals indicates the confusion of the sex-role categories among many.

To take another example, Iroquois, a family of languages spoken in the Northeast Woodlands of North America, differentiates aspects of masculinity and femininity. The examples here are from Mohawk, the easternmost tribe of the Iroquois. While the phonological representation of the actual forms varies from language to language, the system of pronouns remains constant. It is interesting to note that the Iroquois are matrilineal. (The Iroquois pronominals have been described in detail by a number of linguists: Beatty, 1974; Bonvillian 1973; Chafe, 1960, 1967; Lounsbury, 1953). In general, one can hold that the pronominal system distinguishes a singular, dual and plural with first person inclusivity and exclusivity. Furthermore, the third person singular differentiates a masculine, a neuter-zoic and a feminine indefinite. The dual and plural reflect only a masculine and feminine distinction.

In the singular, the masculine pronoun is used largely for human males, although it is also used with animals when one chooses to emphasize that it is a male animal under discussion.

The neuter-zoic form is used for things which are inanimate, non-human animals in general (except as above), and certain women. Although there is some variation in the decision as to which women are included in this category from one dialect to another, generally non-diminutive women and women of child-bearing age who are not relatives of the speaker are included in this category.

The feminine-indefinite category includes small female children (i.e. those below the age of childbearing), small diminutive women (including "little old ladies" above the age of childbearing), and female relatives (e.g. one's own mother). In addition, the feminine indefinite is used for "one" or an indefinite person. "The place where one goes to take out papers" is the translation of the Mohawk (Caughnawaga dialect) word for "post office," but could equally be translated as "The place where she (with respect) goes to take out papers."

The three basic third person forms can all appear with verb stems as in:

rawistos: "he is cold"
kawistos: "she is cold" or "it is cold"
yewistos: "one is cold" or "she (with respect) is cold"

In Mohawk, many words which are translated into English as nouns are in fact verbs. Hence the stem /-uhkwe?-/ "to be human" can be inflected for male and female, giving /ruhkwe?/ "He's a man" or /yuhkwe?/ "She's a woman." (These might be more properly translated as "He's human" and "She's human"). The neuter-zoic form cannot be found prefixed to this stem. The word /ruhkwe?/ is used also for "mankind" (use of "man" is deliberate here) and was used by Mohawks, for example, in translating Expo's title "Man and His World."

Two other forms occur for "man" and "woman" /rohskv?rakehte/ and /tsakotuwisv/ respectively. These two forms, however, are transitive verbs and are marked by the appearance of two pronominal forms /-ro-/ (or /-ho-/ in non-initial position) meaning "He (subject) acts on "him" (object) or "It" (subject) acts on him (object). A possible translation of /rhoskv? rakehte/ suggested by Michaelson (1973) is "warrior" (literally "one who carries a weapon"), although the pronominal structure would seem to imply this is not accurate.

The second pronoun, found in the word for "woman" /-sako-/ (under certain conditions /-hsako-/) is found in other verbals meaning "He (subject) acts on them (object)" or "He (subject) acts on her (object)."

By varying the pronoun on these two words, the more sexual character of these words becomes evident: /thotuwisv/ "male homosexual" and /yohskv?rakehte/ "lesbian" result. The /-yo-/ "It (subject) acts on it (object)" is probably the result of the idea of lesbianism being unnatural, and hence the non-respect forms are used, rather than the plural forms usually used for respect with transitive verbs.

Although the stem used for "male" cannot at this time be translated with any certainty, most Mohawk males indicate that the stem in the word for female has general sexual reference. "It refers to her private parts" said one Mohawk man, while another claimed it to be a verb used to mean "to make heat by friction."

It would seem clear at this point, regardless of the actual segmentation of these forms, that the differences between the stem /-uhkwe?-/ with a female prefix and the stem /-tuwisv-/ imply a rather marked contrast between being a female human and a woman's role sexually. The same distinction appears to hold for the differences between /ruhkwe?/ (male) and /rohskv?rakehte/ (virility).

Given the fact that the role of women in Iroquois has been often stressed, and the fact that Iroquoian seems to be one of the few languages in which an indefinite form is the same as one of the female forms, it is important to note that the term for woman as a transitive verb clearly indicates women are (at least sexually) defined relative to men. The subject position in Iroquois is always filled by the person in the superior status. Further it should be noted that in that relationship, the women are still linguistically marked with the "respect" or "feminine-indefinite" form (i.e. the plural), whereas in the term for lesbian, the form uses the pronouns meaning "neuter-zoic (subject) acts on neuter-zoic (object)."

Let us now return to the categories set up earlier: sex and role. We have said that sex can be seen as the status into which a person is born and is dependent on the set of reproductive organs that are present (either from birth or which are later surgically produced). Sex role refers to the pattern of behavior expected by a society from people born into either of the sex statuses. A subdivision of the sex role is the behavior expected by the society of how a person would behave during the sex act. Sexuality has been used here to refer to how a person performs sexually with members of the opposite sex. It has been indicated that sexuality is a component or aspect of role for males in American society, but not in other societies. What has not yet been discussed is the subdivision of role: How a person behaves during the sex act.

In American culture, behavior during the sex act is a characteristic of role. In general, one may say that men are supposed to be the aggressors, while women are supposed to be passive. In many societies, men must always be above their partners during the sex act (Ford and Beach).

In certain aspects of sexuality there are clear-cut differences between the role itself and the aspect of role. Consider the cases of homosexuality in prisons. It appears that in the world outside of prison, where heterosexual contacts are possible, virility plays a large part in developing and defining a man's masculinity. In most prisons, however, heterosexual contacts are nonexistent. It is at this point that the two aspects of role tend to become crucial. Men in prison tend not to be regarded as homosexuals if they have sex relations with other males; they are regarded as homosexual only if they play a passive role. It is interesting to note that one of the Chinese terms for homosexuals *si fut gwai,* literally "feces hole pervert," can be used to refer to men who are merely passive in social situations and are not necessarily homosexual. In certain subcultures of homosexual male prostutites, boys who are fellated by homosexuals regard themselves as heterosexual. Usually, however, society defines the man's masculinity by his virility. In prison, his willingness to play a "female" role, or even his unwillingness to fight to keep from being forced to play a female role, blocks him from being regarded as male. Prison slang indicates a number of words which are used to distinguish the active versus the passive members of a sex act that occurs between two members of the same sex. This implies that the definition of a homosexual may be even more complex than "a person who actually takes part in a sex act between members of the same sex" or "a person who fantasizes having sex with members of the same sex." Under certain circumstances, a homosexual may be defined by the mode or phases of behavior exhibited during the sex act.

It becomes clear that a number of aspects of sex and role must be distinguished and seen as they integrate with one another before any really comprehensive statement can be made about the variety of roles and statuses that are based on some aspect of sex. In the same way that kinship analysis is needed to identify how the components of the various kinship types are conceived and operate, it is necessary to do the same for systems of terms regarding "sex roles." Cross-cultural analysis is likely to prove extremely valuable and productive in discovering what underlying concepts serve as components in constructing roles.

REFERENCES

ARDREY, R. 1961. African Genesis: A Personal Investigation into the Animal Origins and the Nature of Man. Collins. London.

— 1966. The Territorial Imperative: A Personal Inquiry into the Animal Origins of Property and Nations. Atheneum Press. New York.

BEATTY, J. 1974. Mohawk Morphology. Northern Colorado Press. Greeley, Co.

BONVILLIAN, N. 1973. A Grammar of Akwesasne Mohawk. National Museum of Man, National Museums of Canada. Ottawa, Canada.

CHAFE, W. 1960. Seneca Morphology IJAL Vol 26.

— 1967. Seneca Morphology and Dictionary. Smithsonian Contributions to Anthropology 4, Washington, D.C.

FOX, R. L. Tiger. 1969.

LORENZ, K. 1963. On Aggression. Harcourt Brace and World. New York.

LOUNSBURY, F. 1953. Oneida Verb Morphology. Yale University Publications in Anthropology 48. New Haven, Ct.

MICHELSON, G. 1973. One Thousand Words of Mohawk. National Museum of Man, National Museums of Canada. Ottawa, Canada.

TIGER, L. 1969. Men in Groups. Nelson. London.

Abstract

STYLISTIC STRATEGIES WITHIN A GRAMMAR OF STYLE

ROBIN TOLMACH LAKOFF

Robin Lakoff has extended the model of transformational grammar to a consideration of women's and men's language styles. A crucial assumption of the model is that it accounts not only for production, but also interpretation of others' speech. That is, one uses one's own strategies for transforming meaning into surface representations (sentences) in the interpretation of another's speech. One infers the meaning intended by another speaker by applying one's own transformation routine to the surface representation of the other's speech. Lakoff suggests that males and females differ in their surface styles, and hence in their transformational strategies. These stylistic differences present opportunities for misunderstanding in cross-sex communication.

A scale of style is proposed, based on the degree of relatedness between speaker and hearer. It ranges from *Clarity* at one extreme, the epitome of impersonal speech adopted by newscasters, to *Camaraderie* at the other, which relies heavily on shared knowledge. Next to *Clarity* is *Distance,* the language of professionals in scientific journals, and then *Deference,* which is sensitive to the needs of the listener. Cultures and subcultures (including gender-specific ones) differ in the location of their targeted or normal styles on this scale. Lakoff suggests that the stereotyped American male style lies between *Clarity* and *Distance,* while the stereotyped female style is *Deference.* The gap between the two appears to be narrowing, with males moving toward *Camaraderie* and females toward *Distance.* While equal opportunity for cross-sex misunderstanding exists for both sexes, social factors contribute to an asymetrical interpretation of stylistic differences: female speech is considered deviant, while male speech is taken as normal.

Editors

STYLISTIC STRATEGIES WITHIN A GRAMMAR OF STYLE

Robin Tolmach Lakoff

Department of Linguistics
University of California
Berkeley, California 94720

Interpersonal behavior is frequently regarded as unpredictable and spontaneous. We do not feel that we are following rules or even a preordained pattern in the way we talk to others, move, respond emotionally, work, think—all the varied aspects of what, following Shapiro (1965) we can call personal style. Indeed, some of us might be horrified at the idea that, in *all* our actions, we are governed by implicit rules, just as Chomsky (e.g., 1968) has shown we are in our linguistic behavior (and has thereby himself aroused horrified responses), and are as little aware of it. In this paper, assuming the validity of the assumption of generative grammar that linguistic behavior is rule-governed, I want to extend that claim to a variety of other kinds of behavior that can be subsumed under terms like "character," "personality," or "personal style." I will argue that the same kind of evidence that indicates a need for grammatical rules relating two levels of linguistic structure exists for this wider range of human functioning. Needless to say, the argument that implicit rules guide our behavior denies us neither autonomy nor creativity: these rules are predictive schemata, descriptive rather than prescriptive. In this paper, drawing on previous work, I use as a principal example the distinction between men's and women's typical personal style, in American middle-class culture; but the argument holds for the behavior of any individual or group that is felt by its members and by outsiders to function as a cohesive unit.

The reader may wonder whether there is any justification—beyond my personal whim and the convenience of having previous work to draw upon—for using women's language as a paradigm or model for the purpose of illustrating the more general thesis of the existence of a grammar of style. To this I would make the rejoinder that it is as good as any, and I must choose one. Thus, Chomsky (1965) chose the modal auxiliary system of English as his example attesting to the need for a grammar of the transformational type, although other examples might as well have been used.

But even more to the point, women's language is accessible to every member of this culture as a stereotype. Whether the stereotype is equally valid for all women is certainly debatable; but the fact of its existence, overt or subliminal, affects every one of us and its assumptions are generally agreed on. Hence it provides an especially clear case. And while women's language, and women's style, have long been recognized and commented upon as an aggregate of traits, not much has been done toward accounting for why these particular traits cluster together— that is, toward constructing an explanatory, as opposed to a merely descriptive, mode. I shall attempt a beginning of such a systematization: that is, I shall try to make pre-

53

0077-8923/79/0327-0053 $01.75/2 ©1979, NYAS

dictions, show that there are constraints on co-occurrence, that there are explanations for the existence of some phenomena and the absence of others—in short, to construct a predictive system of rules for style, to establish for style something analogous to what linguists construct for language in the form of a grammar.

To talk really convincingly about style, one should examine *all* aspects of a person's functioning, much as Shapiro investigated several of the aspects of four or five recognized neurotic styles to show how each formed a coherent system, each trait being predictable on the basis of certain postulates. His basic determinant of style was the mode of attentiveness. Obsessive-compulsive style, for instance, involves a need to pay very close attention to small details one at a time, whereas hysterical style works just the opposite way:—a person with such a style perceives the universe as a kind of large undefined blur in which everything is seen at once, and nothing is singled out as outstanding. Shapiro shows how these basic ways of perceiving the world are involved in one's mode of cognition, learning and processing new information; in perception; in ways of using one's body physically; and in one's style of social interaction. This interaction, like the grammar of a language one speaks, is something the normal participant knows about unconsciously or implicitly. So, seeing that X is concerned with details in his work, seldom looking at the larger issues but confining himself to tiny aspects of the problem, an observer will expect, consciously or otherwise, to find that X is very precise in his linguistic expression, that he will be very concerned with using just the right word, and that he is apt to be conservative, politically and socially, feeling uncomfortable with surprises of any sort. We can then informally state, as a rule, "If there is concern for details, then there will be avoidance of surprises." If this is borne out in future encounters with X, and, further, with Z and W, the observer feels comfortable—his rule works, he is in control. If, on the other hand, X—or W, or Z—turns out to be flighty in his political affiliations and fuzzy in his choice of expression, the observer may be puzzled, and may feel and or even remark to others that that person is a paradox, you can not figure him out. Similarly, if the observer finds that X on one occasion is bound up with niggling details, he comes to expect this sort of behavior of X on subsequent occasions, and will likewise be surprised if on their next meeting X affects an extremely general and undefined *Weltanschauung*. So our rules are predictive across modalities (that is, from one aspect of behavior to another) as well as across time (from one encounter to the next). I will call these predictabilities by the names, respectively, of *coherency* and *consistency,* and assume that for something to be recognized as a personal style it must possess both these attributes. (I assume that personal style may, as a result of the vicissitudes of life, through conscious motivation or otherwise, change in several of its salient aspects over time, but typically rather slowly and not too radically. I leave open here the question of how much style—or character, or personality—may really change.)

Stylistic coherency, then, is the predictability of one component of personal style from another, on the basis of more or less apparent similarities between them, genetically or dynamically. This notion, as I suggested above, is reminiscent of the basic linguistic concept of co-occurrence as a criterion for grammaticality. Syntactic rules tell us, among other things, which words, or other elements, may occur side by side with others. If these constraints are violated an uninterpretable, or at least unacceptable, sentence results. Such a constraint may involve semantic criteria, as in the well-known example

(1) Colorless green ideas sleep furiously

in which the problems arise because semantic categories are juxtaposed contrary to universal meaning constraints. They may also involve syntactic criteria, as in

(2) John will leave for Rome yesterday

where the use of the future tense conflicts with the use of *yesterday,* referring to past time, or

(3) The boys is here

Of course, we might as legitimately call the last two semantic violations, illustrating a fact that most linguistic theorists have come to accept, with sorrow: levels of grammar cannot be dealt with as separable entities. We are dealing with parallel problems when we want to define normal style. Thus, we would like to express, in precise and possibly even formal notation (an attempt that has been made in linguistic theory for some time, and though it has never really been successful, it has been valuable as a learning experience for linguists), the intuitively correct generalization that certain modalities of human behavior can be reasonably expected to co-occur, and others cannot. As an example, within the linguistic sphere of style alone, we can state a few co-occurrence constraints:

(a) A person given to pontification on large and abstract issues of great universal and philosophical relevance, most likely, will employ an elaborately Latinate and convoluted vocabulary as well as a rather Germanic syntax wherewith to express these thoughts: there is an expected co-occurrence of lexical, syntactic, and semantic material.

(b) A person given to asking questions where others might use declaratives can be expected also to employ euphemistic modes of speech on any topic that might be embarrassing, and might further engage in a lot of linguistic hedging (I guess; sorta; y'know). Here we find co-occurrence of syntactic and lexical patterns.

Exceptions occur, of course, but we tend to remember them particularly as they are so striking. ("Mary is so polite whenever she wants you to do anything; how come she uses four-letter words?") Such exceptions, notable and memorable as they may be, are the exception rather than the rule, comparable to the uses of poets who employ locutions like "A grief ago," or "the fog comes in on little cat feet," thereby violating the rules of linguistic co-occurrence discussed previously, and thereby creating particularly memorable strings of words, typically called "poetry." I do not want to imply that such stylistic incompatibilities are subsumable under the rubric of behavioral poetry; but it is perhaps not beside the point to suggest that, when extreme, they are assigned to a special category to which there is given a special name, namely "schizophrenia." The relationship between schizophrenic behavior and poetic behavior is frequently if inadequately commented upon by workers in many fields.

Additionally, co-occurrence constraints on style pertain between different modalities:

(A) Someone who dresses conservatively and very carefully can be expected to use language carefully and equally precisely.

(B) Someone who divides humanity into black and white also, cognitively, divides ideas into right and wrong, with no gray areas in either case. Again, there are people who violate these expectations, but they are experienced as aberrant. If the aberration is clearly purposeful, for effect, it is comic: much of Woody Allen's humor, for example, depends on incompatibilities of stylistic modalities. But if it seems unintentional, we consider it indicative of serious psychopathology—schizophrenia again.

Co-occurrence constraints are but one aspect of grammatical rules. Syntactic theory devised over the last couple of decades makes other assumptions about human linguistic capacities, capacities that are assumed on the basis of excellent evidence to be found in all human languages. We might well ask how far to carry the generalization. We know that language is a form of communication of thoughts and emotions, perhaps (though not certainly) the form of communication *par excellence*. But there are other modes employed by normal persons. Language is surely the principal conscious and intentional mode; but that does not mean it is the most important or the most frequent or the best-understood. Rather, all sorts of arguments and evidence have been adduced of late that language is but a sort of frosting on the cake; when conflict exists between what a speaker is expressing linguistically and what he is communicating, generally unintentionally, by means of other modalities, other participants in the communication tend, generally unconsciously, to interpret the nonlinguistic communication as the genuine or truthful one.[1] But to say this is to assume that, not only do these sophisticated interpreters of discourse (i.e., you and I and everyone else) employ their implicit rules in the interpretation of *linguistic* structures (as we have been perfectly well aware for quite some time), but that we use the same system for what is sometimes called extralinguistic or paralinguistic functioning, and we detect mismatches by our application of these rules. Woe betide anyone caught in a mismatch (Richard Nixon is a notorious example). I take it, then, as proved that nonlinguistic style is as much rule governed behavior as is linguistic style, and I would further venture—it is not yet proved by any means—that the same kinds of rules, the same basic devices, are operative in all human behavioral systems. Style is a unity, not only in its superficial manifestations in the normal individual, but also in its basic mechanisms.

---

[1] The work of Paul Ekman is particularly interesting in this regard, indicating that subjects, when forced to decide between conflicting interpretations of a contribution based on facial expression and verbal statement, will opt for the truth of the former.

It is therefore incumbent on the linguist determined to give evidence for this last contention to show that those traits ascribed to the linguistic grammar can be justified and indeed are essential as parts of a wider stylistic grammar. If this should be provable, we can be content in that we have given yet another instance of the working of Occam's razor: after all, doesn't it make sense that the human mind should function with as little baggage as it can get away with? If it can be shown to need only one general rule system, from which all forms of psychic behavior can be derived, isn't this preferable to a theory that requires separate theories, and thus separate rules, for each subtype of behavior? But even if the former is ideal, it naturally remains to be proved. I do not intend to make a watertight case for psychic economy here, but merely to give some preliminary arguments showing that a unified system is tenable. I use linguistic theory as my template, and more specifically a kind of generalized theory derived from various realizations of generative grammar. The reason I do so is partly that I am trained as a linguist, so it comes naturally to me, but also because it is the only attempt at formalization of psychic structure that I know, the only attempt, I should say, at a predictive rather than a merely taxomonic or classificatory framework, such as are found in many psychological theories of character.

To return to the point: linguistic theory assumes a bipartite syntax (here I am oversimplifying considerably, but the complexities are not important for our purposes). In such a syntactic model, two levels of syntactic structure are relevant: a superficial level, which is the utterance as it appears in spoken or written form; and the underlying or deep structure, which is related to the meaning of the sentence, and contains in a form accessible to inspection all the elements needed to account for the meaning of the sentence. Since every sentence in a language that is found in superficial form can be related to an underlying form, we must assume a set of transformational rules, relating these two levels, explaining formally the relation between the sentence as it appears on the surface and what it "means." For often, if we are asked what a sentence means, how its component parts are related, to answer that question properly we will have to refer to elements that are not present on the surface, but can be inferred from the properties of the rest of the sentence. It is frequently assumed that transformational rules exist to make sentences easier to understand or quicker to utter; this is true some of the time, although by no means always.[2] So if we want to argue for parallelism between linguistic and other levels of psychic functioning, we shall have to give evidence for these two levels in stylistic behavior, and a set of rules linking them, stating, for instance, in effect, that Surface Structure A always corresponds to Underlying Structure B, through the application of Transformational Rule C.

---

[2] Arguments for transformational rules as processing strategies were first advanced by Bever and Langendoen in their 1972 paper, "The interaction of speech perception and grammatical structure in the evolution of language," in *Linguistic Change and Generative Theory,* R.P. Stockwell & R.K.S. Macaulay, Eds. Indiana University Press, Bloomington, Ind.

The most persuasive evidence for this duality of stucture in language is in the existence of ambiguity and paraphrase relationships between sentences, which could not otherwise be explained. A sentence is ambiguous if it has different meanings depending on the contexts in which it is uttered: such a surface structure can be explained as being related by two different transformational routes to two different underlying structures. So for instance with (4):

(4) Visiting relatives can be a nuisance.

In one derivational history, we start from an underlying structure roughly equivalent in meaning to (5) —not itself an underlying structure:

(5) Relatives who visit can be a nuisance.

and in the other, to (6):

(6) For one to visit relatives can be a nuisance.

In each of these underlying structures, something is deleted to produce the superficial sentence (4), but in each case something different is deleted. Hence, starting from structures with different meanings, we end up with identical structures.

On the other hand, sometimes we find two quite different superficial sentences that are very similar in meaning. Such sentences are paraphrases of one another. Examples (7) and (8), and (9) and (10) are illustrative.

(7) The ball was hit by the boy.

(8) The boy hit the ball.

(9) John threw the garbage out.

(10) John threw out the garbage.

The members of each pair originate as very similar underlying structures, but they undergo different sets of transformational rules, leading to two different superficial representations. Since the underlying structures of each pair are closely similar, the meanings of the sentences in each pair are similar as well; the surface forms are different because each has a different syntactic history.[3] Just as the existence of these types of relationships in grammar is evidence for the duality of grammatical structures, if we could find evidence of a similar duality in other modalities of human behavior, we would have persuasive evidence that a similar duality should be postulated to explain these other modalities.

I have given evidence elsewhere (1977) of the existence of such relationships. To summarize, I have suggested that women's language and (typically male) academese function for the same underlying or deeper purpose, that of evading responsibility for what is being said; but they do it by different superficial means, which incidentally are given very different values by our culture; and these then are essentially paraphrases of one another, like the examples of sentences (7) — (10) above; and that women's style and children's style, although superficially similar in many of their aspects, are actually used with rather different aims and arise from very different

---

[3] I am oversimplifying greatly here, and probably distorting the facts more than I ought. The basic premise is true, but the discussion of the intricacies involved in the differences of meaning and usage in the members of each pair, however valid, would take us far afield.

psychic situations, so that they can be said to have different meanings, different underlying structures, corresponding to similar surface structures, and thus are stylistically ambiguous. These arguments imply that many if not all the modalities of human behavior are dualistic in their functioning, and therefore, are best interpreted as governed by rules at the least analogous to, and perhaps identical to, the kinds of rules that have been identified as existing in linguistic structures.

We can in fact give arguments that, in the various aspects of human style, there are analogous processes to those of language. Linguistic rules are implicit, or unconscious: a speaker follows them, using them to produce as well as to distinguish grammatical utterances of his language without being able to state the form of these rules, and typically without even knowing that such rules exist. Linguists know that there exists a syntactic rule relating sentences like (8) and (9); but even linguists, with their special knowledge, cannot give the correct form of this rule; "naïve speakers," even worse off in this respect, may be interested to learn in an elementary syntax course that they have access to such rules. Yet the naïve speaker has no trouble using and processing passive sentences. Similarly we correlate the various aspects of our style, we determine whether or not a new piece of behavior on the part of an acquaintance surprises us, we decide whether the range of a person's behaviors in the course of an evening or a month or a year is reasonable fluctuation or evidence of serious psychopathology; we do all this on the basis of some internal mechanism, a predictive device that we may perfectly accurately refer to as a grammar of style, a set of stylistic rules. (It should not be necessary to point out that these unconscious rules, linguistic and behavioral, are descriptive and predictive, rather then prescriptive: they tell us, in effect, what will be encountered on the basis of what has been found, rather than telling us what we ought to do to act right.) In talking informally about behavior, we make reference to distinctions between intention and execution, or intention and perception, which are analogous to the underlying/superficial structure dichotomy of linguistics.

Linguistics as a scientific methodology has very real relevance to the methods of the other social sciences. While it is true that they have achieved far more success with quantification of their data than has linguistics, lending credence to the notion that that the latter is unscientifically soft-nosed, nonetheless linguistics alone among the social sciences has attempted to represent the data it uncovers in terms of formal rules—predictive and simplifying generalizations. While generative grammar has not been tremendously successful in writing rules that actually work, nonetheless, we recognize that mechanisms of the sorts devised by theorists in this field must exist and will ultimately function as we might desire. But linguistics illustrates for other social sciences the importance of devising grammars, predictive rather than merely taxonomic models. So when I speak of a grammar of style, I mean that we are to transfer the concepts devised for linguistic theory—rules, co-occurrence constraints, ungrammaticality, and so forth— to the description of other forms of human behavior, a system that if adequate will not only categorize what is actually extant, but will also indicate what does not exist, in normal persons on the one hand, and in general on the other.

With this definition in mind, let us turn to the examination of stylistic behavior. I have said that, to be a style, behavior must be able to be seen as both coherent across modalities and consistent across time, and that one form of stylistic pathology may lie in the failure to be either coherent or consistent, or both. Further, a style assumes a match between dual levels of structure—the one that is superficially accessible to participants in an interaction, and the other, the level of intention, which itself may be multileveled and accessible not at all or in varying degrees to participants in their interactions. Also, participants generally assume a one-to-one relationship between intention and execution: if I perform Behavior A, my interlocutor is apt to assume that I have intended to communicate B. There is some possibility for ambiguity, even as there is in language, but as with language, in actual practice the context, for normal individuals, tends to disambiguate most potential ambiguities. So for instance if a female participant does something others will interpret it one way; if a male, another—since "female" and "male" are different contexts. As also with language, some users are much better at realizing that two readings might exist, and determining which is the one that is correct in that context. And the fact that many people apparently are not capable of doing this efficiently causes great difficulty in interpersonal relationships—difficulty that is particularly troublesome because participants are seldom aware of its cause, or even of its precise form.

While Shapiro described one contributor to style—the nature and degree of attentiveness—style has many other potential points of differentiation. We could think of it as a grid, with Shapiro's distinctions being one column of many. This makes sense, in that we do not typically consider a person completely classified when we have labeled him or her, as, say, hysterical or obsessive-compulsive. We also define such an individual as demure or assertive; as reticent or loquacious; and so forth *ad infinitum*. Another point of differentiation is the mode of rapport: the relative importance for the individual of making the content of the communication clear, versus establishing a personal relationship with others, where this choice must be made; and, where the latter is determined to be important, how rapport is to be effected, what mode of presentation of self the individual chooses to adopt. There are obvious correlations between Shapiro's attentiveness-oriented and my rapport-oriented categorizations, so that the grammar should allow us to predict one category of behavior from another: e.g., someone who tends toward diffuse attentiveness is apt to display rapport-related behavior. But on the other hand, a person whose attention tends to be highly constricted and confined will impress others as being unwilling to establish rapport.

Shapiro talks about these relationships, in fact, noting that hysterical characters, people utilizing diffuse attentiveness, tend toward a quick if shallow emotional rapport, the appearance of intimacy; while a contrastive type, obsessive-compulsive characters, tend toward impersonal relationships and aloof politeness. But we should like to know why this is so; what it is in the individual that necessitates these co-occurrence relationships, which we assume are not coincidental. I am suggesting that Shapiro's taxonomies can be expressed as parts of a grammar, i.e., made into a predictive system. We want to explain *why* we encounter these juxtapositions and not others, as character types. And while extremes of these two types are far from "normal," and may even be considered psychotic at the farthest reaches, they are found.

In another way too character style is reminiscent in its logic of linguistic grammar. Looking at language, we can place any string of words on a scale, from "fully grammatical, normal, and acceptable," like (11) through "intelligible but peculiar," like (12), to "bizarre and uninterpretable, meaningless," like (13).

(11) The boy hit the ball.

(12) Won't you please get the hell out of here.

(13) Two boys elapsed.

The determination as to whether the sentences are acceptable and meaningful, or the degree to which they are so judged, rests on the co-occurrence relations of items in the sentence. In (11), there is no problem. In (12), we have a pragmatic conflict: "please" correlates with social situations in which we are trying to be polite and gentle, "the hell" with contexts where we are willing to be brusque and rude, and so it is in some sense inappropriate for both to occur together. But the meaning of the sentence is not impaired, only its emotional content. In (13), however, a concrete noun serves as subject for the verb *elapse,* which semantically can refer only to abstract subjects, and more specifically, expressions of time (cf. the perfectly appropriate and intelligble, *Two hours elapsed.*) The breaking of co-occurrence constraints in (13) is analogous to that in (12), but of a deeper and more serious order, affecting meaning.

Character types, too, may reasonably be looked at as linguists interpret sentences: the more bizarre a personality seems to us, the more serious is the violation of the stylistic co-occurrence rules that creates it. So (11) is similar to a more or less normal person in terms of the interplay of relevant characteristics: (12) to, let us say, a hysteric—we are not quite sure what to make of the behavior, it is not what we expect, but we can learn to make allowances; (13), to a schizophrenic, whose behavior may be totally uninterpretable, and frightening to us as the hysteric's is not, for just that reason.

Further, just as with linguistic rules, we have an implicit notion of stylistic rules and recognize when they are violated, even though we usually are at a loss to say what it is that we recognize. Perhaps the most striking instance of this unconscious recognition of character co-occurrence is found in literature: in the novel, and perhaps most crucially in drama. What distinguishes a good novelist or playwright, as well as a good actor or director, perhaps above all else, is the creation of credible characters. And what we mean by "credible" has largely to do with the co-occurrence of stylistic traits, traits drawn from the repertoire of the personality as a whole. A writer, a director, and an actor probably perceive this intuitive coherence in different ways, or at least make different use of their intuitions: but what distinguishes the great from the second-rate is an almost uncanny sense of which combinations are plausible, which not.

These observations that I have made on style can be described in terms of a theory of communicative competence such as I have discussed in somewhat different form elsewhere (1977). What is relevant to the present discussion is the part of the system that describes how participants determine the appropriate mode of presentation of self in discourse with others, on the basis of their own personal habits, the relationship between participants, and the subject matter under discussion. On the basis of this intuitive judgment, the speaker selects—fluent speakers, generally unconsciously—a matching strategy, dictating the point on the scale shown in FIGURE 1 that is deemed appropriate by the speaker's subculture for the type of interaction in which the speaker assesses himself or herself to be engaged. It is the Rules of Communicative Competence that enable speakers to make judgments as to the use and interpretation of sentences. And, like the latter, the implicit Rules I am describing here function as models both for production and interpretation of the contributions of others, so that—a significant point, as we shall see later—one understands the contributions of others only in terms of one's own internalized strategies. But it is important to bear in mind that the named points on the continuum represent strategies, or modalities, of interaction, rather than Rules: the rules themselves, then, can be seen as meta-strategies. The modalities themselves, and the relationships among them, are universal; but the statement of the Rules about which point is appropriate in a particular context—as well as the decision as to how the context itself is to be interpreted—differs from culture to culture as well as from individual to individual. These differences are the basic determinants of personal style. The strategies themselves and their interrelationships can be expressed in schematic form as in FIGURE 1.

CLARITY ⟶ DISTANCE ⟶ DEFERENCE ⟶ CAMARADERIE

least relationship   most relationship
between participants   between participants

FIGURE 1.

The strategies are named in terms of the kind of relationship each assumes as ideal. The relationship-based continuum illustrated as FIGURE 1 correlates with Shapiro's model, enabling us, for instance, to superimpose the characteristic linguistic preferences which this theory of Communicative Competence presupposes upon Shapiro's attentiveness continuum. To speak of a continuum from least to most explicit relationship between speakers is not to imply that necessarily, when one strategy is selected by the participant as appropriate, they disavow entirely the extistence of any sort of relationship between them indicated by another strategy. What is at issue is what is explicit—whether or not the speaker affirms, by something in the communication proper (whether strictly linguistic or not)—that there is another person involved in the discourse, not just the facts that are being communicated themselves.

The continuum represents, from left to right, an increasing awareness of the addressee's presence as explicitly manifested by the speaker. A situation requiring Clarity will entail a rather colorless contribution: lexical items will be selected that are emotionally drab and associated with the deliberative or consultative registers of speech: neither oratorical, nor poetic, nor slang—essentially safe speech, which does not identify its speaker as a particular and individual human being, and which does not make any overt assumptions about the character or needs of the addressee. So the participants themselves are not made noticeable: the message itself, the information conveyed, is what is important, and the aim of Clarity-based discourse is to express this information as clearly and succinctly as possible. H.P. Grice's Conversational Maxims (1975) can be thought of as exemplary of the expectations of ideal behavior in this framework (though not, as we shall see, under other assumptions). So when Clarity is involved, there is no indirectness, circumlocution, or redundancy.

Clarity is often thought of as the ideal mode of discourse, at least in this culture at the present time. Hence there has been a great deal written popularly of late bemoaning its apparent demise: it is claimed that people are becoming less able to speak and write clearly, and it is generally assumed that it really is a matter of inability, that people would express themselves in accordance with Clarity if only they could think clearly, as they used to be able to do. But as I have argued elsewhere (1976), in fact the reason that people do not communicate directly and forcefully is that they do not choose to; that such a mode of expression is no longer viewed as indicative of our culture's good human being; that, given the choice between seeming (to oneself as well as others) fuzzy-minded and seeming impersonal, most contemporary speakers would opt for the former. But at the same time, older standards, still in force, assert that the person who does not speak in accordance with Clarity is not to be taken seriously, at least in a professional milieu. So conflicts arise, which are seldom completely conscious.

The crucial question is what people view as the main aim of an interaction. If, as is frequently assumed, the transmission of factual or real-world information is the ultimate purpose of any linguistic discourse, we would have to make some rather surprising judgments. Since Clarity is the only mode of communicative competence that is specifically concerned with the transmission of information, and since only what is transmitted in conformity with the statements of Clarity is maximally informative, we would, given such an assumption, have to view any failure to use Clarity as a bizarre, unintelligible, or pointless contribution. And we would find that a very large percentage of conversations fell into this category. What we discover in fact is that only a relatively few contexts are appropriate for Clarity-based contributions, and that anyone who makes use of Clarity under other conditions, or at any rate does so persistently, is considered—not a particularly admirable member of the culture, still less an extremely effective communicator—but rather, someone distinctly aberrant, or at worst psychotic. We obviously have to rethink the notion that being clear is always best, or even always good.

Distance, the next discrete point to the right, appears to invite even more impersonality than does Clarity, but only superficially. When Clarity enjoins us to "Be clear," Distance says "Remain aloof." But to talk of aloofness and distancing is to assume that the relationship between the participants is of interest, even if that relationship consists of statying as far apart as possible. So the use of this strategy ensures that participants will tread on each other's toes as little as possible—and therefore assumes each has toes to be trodden on. Here we find formal politeness, the rules of etiquette, diplomatic language, bureaucratese and professional jargons of all kinds—all sytems designed to maximize the distance between the participants—and at the same time, to impute authority to the speaker, whether through status or expertise. Hence what is being communicated is particularly hard for anyone else to question. While Clarity is unemotional, Distance is anti-emotional: the form of expression is chosen partly on the grounds that there is something covertly present in the intended communication that may be unpleasantly emotion-provoking and therefore needs to be neutralized by the speaker. On the other hand, Clarity assumes that participants are dealing with cold facts, and there is nothing to conceal. So as Clarity is the language of news broadcasts and classroom lectures, Distance is the mode of communication of the more defensive—the politician, the bureaucrat, the academic delivering a paper. Both Clarity and Distance lend an air of uninvolvement to a communication.

Distance uses technical terminology, formal polite language, and overly correct diction and grammar—the opposite of the colloquial. All this makes it hard to understand, precisely because we do some of our intellectual understanding through our emotions, and the denial of emotionality makes it very hard for us to figure out what really is being said, and how we ought to respond to it. Because of the safety in Distance, people are more apt to lapse into it the more they are afraid of the repercussions of what they are saying, whether because they fear what they say is unpopular, or because it may be incorrect. Distance is, furthermore, a means of avoiding responsibility for what one is saying, while claiming the authority and power necessary to say it. So bureaucratese and its relatives frequently make those who are exposed to them nervous, much though their users seek to placate—or rather, narcotize. And the use of Distance, since it implies that the speaker holds power over the person addressed, is abrasive as the other modalities are not.

Deference too establishes a relationship between participants. But this modality explicitly recognizes the existence of both participants and their relationship, where Clarity ignores these issues and Distance denies them. Using Deference, the speaker is following the injunction: "Don't impose—give options." Thus, its use implies that decisions as to the interpretation and outcome of the exchange are in the hands of the addressee, whether actually or merely conventionally. Even if the deference is mere convention, however, the very fact that the speaker chooses to adopt that convention is a mark of courtesy, as most people prefer conventional deference to outright and real brusqueness. Deference apparently leaves the important decisions up to the addressee—although the speaker really knows perfectly well what he intends to achieve by his contribution, and gives plenty of instructions overtly or covertly to the addressee to indicate the desired response. In fact, sometimes the use of Deference creates friction between participants precisely because the speaker seems to be giving with one hand and taking with another, offering autonomy but in fact retaining power as instanced by the very ability to *offer* autonomy. Then the addressee is often faced with the impossible task of determining which of the levels of communication to recognize—the overt offer, or the covert injunction? Either way is risky. Where Distance avoids uncomfortable topics by the pretense of intellectual uninvolvement, that is, by denying the emotive force of the contribution, Deference denies the cognitive content, conventionally of course (or else understanding could not take place), saying in effect, "It's up to you to translate my message: if you decide we're talking about THAT, we are." Hence euphemism is characteristic of this modality.

Camaraderie, necessitating as it does direct confrontation, is the modality least in accord with what we usually think of as "politeness." For Camaraderie explicitly acknowledges that a relationship exists and is important, whether one of friendliness or of hostility. Camaraderie is the level of direct expression of orders and desires, colloquialism and slang, first names and nicknames—much that is considered good and typical contemporary American behavior.

The strategies have been described as points on a continuum partly because they can be used in isolation or in combination: a contribution can be pure-Distance, or mostly Distance, with a little Deference, or half of each. Some people are very formal, distant, and aloof; others less so; still others, hardly at all. FIGURE 1, however, makes some combinational possibilities hard to visualize: a situation such as that exemplified in FIGURE 2 is no problem—a style falling between Distance and Deference, which are contiguous,

---

CLARITY —— DISTANCE —X— DEFERENCE ——CAMARADERIE

FIGURE 2.

but this diagram would make it impossible to represent, say, a combination of Distance and Camaraderie, which is just as theoretically possible. One way of avoiding these difficulties in FIGURE 3, with the left-right axis maintained intact, but some means of indicating that combinations between any of the modalities are possible. We still cannot graphically represent combinations of three and four modalities, but FIGURE 3 is at least a step toward more accurate representation. A specific linguistic entity—whether a lexical item, an intonation pattern, or a syntactic formula—is typically categorizable as assigned to one of the named points on our diagram, while the overall stylistic behavior on the part of individuals can fall at nodal points or between them. So FIGURE 1 can still be thought of as an appropriate model for the subcomponents of which style is composed, but FIGURE 3 seems a better representation of a style as a whole.

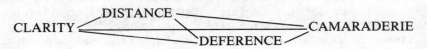

FIGURE 3.

As an example of the operation of this system, let us examine the differences between women's and men's ideal styles in this culture. It is important to remember at the outset that, when two types of behavior are put in contrast by a society, they will tend to be polarized—to be perceived and stereotyped as more different than they probably are. But these exaggerated stereotypes must, to be intelligible, be based on real differences.

Let us think for convenience of people who typify our masculine and feminine idealizations—say, Clark Gable or Marilyn Monroe, who perhaps seem particularly exemplary to us now since we have had time to abstract their images from reality. If we were to place these people—in their official Hollywood personalities—on our chart, I think we would place Gable somewhere on the Clarity-Distance axis, and Monroe along Deference-Camaraderie—about as far away from each other as they could be. Gable is perceived as the strong, silent type—he says just as much as necessary to get information across, and is somehow withdrawn into himself, almost reclusive. Think of Rhett Butler saying, "Frankly, my dear, I don't give a damn," as the epitome of the ideal masculine style that most of us have come to maturity assuming. When such a man speaks, his contribution is incisive, precise, and to the point—utterly straightforward—and tells us as little as possible about the speaker's state of mind and his attitude toward the addressee. We expect here, too, an even and low pitch, flat intonation, declarative rather than interrogative sentence structure, no hedging or imprecision, and lexical items chosen for their pure cognitive content, not their emotional coloration. If such a person shows emotion, it will be anger rather than tenderness or grief. Anger is expressed, ideally, not by raising the loudness or pitch of the voice, but by becoming ever more precise, softspoken, withdrawn—an exaggeration of the silent characteristics. As a contemporary example of the type, we can think of Walter Cronkite, at least in his public person. Not for nothing is he the "most trusted man in America." He is trusted because his style is the very epitome of the current ideal. Cronkite's style is probably perceived as somewhat closer to Clarity than Distance on the scale, where Gable's was the reverse, but they are otherwise similar.

By contrast, Monroe's public presentation of self was profoundly imprecise. There is always a sense that the audience does not really know what she is talking about (nor does she), but that she is very concerned with whomever she is talking to, concerned with whether he is interested in her, and whether his needs are being met. Here we have the reverse of Gable-Cronkite style: Clarity is entirely absent, and there is no evidence of Distancing behavior. In contrast to Gable's characteristic poker face, we have Monroe either smiling or looking sensuous, but certainly wearing an identifiable facial expression. She uses interjections and hedges freely and her dialog is sprinkled with "I guess" and "kinda" in distinction to Gable's unembellished "yup's." Her sentences seem not to end, but rather to be elliptical, as if in invitation to the addressee to finish them for her—classic feminine deference.

These diverse styles are also classifiable on Shapiro's scale —Gable/Cronkite's as representative of obsessive-compulsive style, Monroe's of what Shapiro terms hysterical. More accurately, we would want to place truly neurotic examples of stylistic behavior farther along our lines than any of these more or less normal examples, but certainly it is arguable that this culture's paradigmatic masculine style shares a great many traits with a "neurotic" obsessive-compulsive style; and our prototypical example of femininity is exemplary in many of its aspects of neurotic hysterical style. Shapiro shows too how the communicative behaviors I have just discussed correlate with cognitive, perceptual and motoric forms of functioning to produce the coherency we call personal style.

Now we are faced with some interesting observations. I have remarked that those linguistic traits that are characteristic of men in our society correlate with a form of functioning that verges on the obsessive-compulsive; and, feminine traits correlate with hysterical behavior. It is a truism among psychological theorists that hysterical traits of character are predominantly found in women, so that it has sometimes been thought they were exclusively the province of women. And similarly though less strikingly a correlation has been claimed between obsessive-compulsive style and masculine behavior.

Students of style in general, and linguistic behavior more specifically, have tended to talk in terms of women's behavior, women's style—as opposed to a more general notion, people's style. Women have always been classified as the other, the not-quite-human, whether by medieval theologians who claimed women had no souls, or by more modern psychologists (as demonstrated in the Broverman, 1970, study) who would claim that a "healthy woman" and a "healthy man" are characterologically very different things: a "healthy man" is identified with a "healthy human being" or "healthy person," while a "healthy woman" is not. This extremely dangerous prejudice infects much of our scholarly behavior implicitly or explicitly. There is nothing wrong with talking about women's style or women's language as long as it is not covertly opposed to "everyone's style" or "normal language." The chart I have sketched indicates quite clearly that both the prototypically masculine and prototypically feminine variants of stylistic behavior are representable as points at one or another end of the continuum; each is equally far from the ideal middle, or norm, which presumably is rather rare in actuality. We have several prejudices to overcome here: that women's special manifestations are further from the norm than men's, which in this system of thought *is* the norm; and that anything nonnormal and hence nonmasculine is worse, weaker, or degenerate. Both of these covert (sometimes embarrassingly overt) assumptions color our perceptions of the stylistic differences in the behavior of the sexes. If indeed we are brainwashed into believing that anything on the Deference-Camaraderie end is no good, we will object strenuously to the very idea that there is a women's style, distinct from men's. But if we can see that there is no difference in degree or validity between behavior at the two ends of the continuum, perhaps we can study both as interesting entities. In the same way our society rewards behavior on the "masculine" or obsessive-compulsive side as being in keeping with the work ethic, logical thought, and so on and disavows the other end as irrational, lazy, or nonserious. It is common to counter these attacks by claiming the difference does not exist; but there is another way, to say that it does but that neither side constitutes the more virtuous human being. Further, both sides could gain from moving a bit closer to the center at least some of the time.

It seems rather natural, indeed inescapable, that neurotic characteristics should pattern as they do: for obsessive-compulsive style is merely an exaggeration of our culture's preferred masculine mode of presention of self; and similarly, hysterical style is an exaggeration of the feminine.[4] We might say that neurotic behavior is not just randomly aberrant behavior; but rather, one tends to become neurotic by exaggerating and calcifying the mode of response to the environment one would be using normally. As Shapiro and others define neurosis as inflexibility in adjusting behavior to the environment, this reasoning seems to make sense. Then it further follows that more women will be classified as neurotic than will men, since neurosis is defined as departure from a preferred norm; and the norm is defined in terms of masculine behavior. So for a man to be diagnosed as obsessive-compulsive, he must exaggerate those characteristics even beyond how a man (i.e., a healthy human being) in this culture is supposed to display them: but to be a hysterical woman, one need only be a "good"

---

[4] It is true that obsessive-compulsive style is more prevalent among women than hysterical style is, or has ever been, among men. As far as I know, no reason for this is advanced in the literature dealing with neurosis. One possible line of explanation is suggested here: if neurosis is another term for the inflexible adherence to a cultural target, it makes more sense to cling to a target that is given some respectability, than one which is ridiculed. There is a sort of hierarchy, perhaps, in the selection of a neurotic style: first, choose the one that is the exaggeration of one's own group's preferred strategy; failing that, for whatever reason, choose what is culturally valued. So a woman would most naturally select hysteria, second, obsessional neurosis. A man presumably has only the latter option.

woman—the more hysterical, the better. But the better a hysteric, the worse a human being by the androcentric definition of that term. By this reasoning, a woman finds herself stylistically in a double bind. She cannot be rewarded at once for being feminine and being human as a man can for being both masculine and human. It is a problem, and really not *her* problem, but her culture's (Lakoff, 1975).

We can say, then, that a culture has implicitly in its collective mind a concept of how a good human being should behave: a *target* for its members to aim at and judge themselves and others by. Members of the culture over the age of adolescence (perhaps earlier; in the past, certainly earlier)—at least male members—are expected to behave accordingly. Outsiders, marked typically by their accented speech, a badge of outsiderhood, are excused from some of the rules, although the behavior of members of other societies is nonetheless judged by the criteria of the culture doing the judging: thus we may say, for instance, that the Japanese are "deferential," i.e., employ the rule of Deference more than a male in our culture would, and the Germans are "arrogant," meaning more or less that they use Distance more than we would. We get impressions of foreigners as if they were members of our own culture. So rather than saying to ourselves (unconsciously, of course), "Although he presents the appearance of arrogance, I don't consider him arrogant because that is normal behavior within the context of being a German, which he is," we say, "He's arrogant, but that's what I expect from someone who speaks with a German accent; they don't know any better, so I'll overlook it." While superficially this may seem to be a hairsplitting distinction, it has considerable import, especially as regards feelings about feminine behavior.

For just as German are aliens in the American culture, because they have a different target for relating to others, so are women in this male-centered or androcentric culture which identifies "healthy human beinghood" with the masculine stereotype. Woman are the *other,* just as surely as are Germans or Japanese, and are similarly stereotyped in joke and folklore: women are fuzzy-minded, women are not precise, women are overly polite and careful in their speech and actions. We have no comparable stereotypes for men, even as we have no jokes based on stereotypical male behavior (analogous to "woman driver" or "mother-in-law" jokes) nor expectations based on necessarily male roles. (Compare the prevalence of assumptions about widows, or for that matter divorcees, in our culture past and present, with that of widowers and divorced men. It is significant that the spoken form "divorcé(e)" will almost certainly, unless clearly disambiguated by context, be interpreted as feminine.)

I have already mentioned the paradox that a woman cannot at once be a healthy woman and a healthy human being: the stylistic ideals are directly contradictory. There is an additional problem as well, deriving from another stereotypical view of women prevalent through the ages: women are manipulative, deceitful, do not say what they mean; people cannot figure them out, they do not play by the rules. Whether or not this stereotyping is fair, whether it represents reality, is not relevant here. It is important, however, to acknowledge the prevalence of this stereotype, in our culture and throughout the world. To change it, we must understand its prevalence, and give a reason why people (including many women) have clung to it so tenaciously. It is convenient because it represents still another way in which women are categorized as "the other, the non-human." For we do not have an analogous deleterious stereotype of men, although parallels could no doubt be constructed. But the crucial question is whether there lurks a reality behind the stereotype. For stereotypes are important to study only insofar as they are representations of reality. And I would argue further that societies only create and maintain those stereotypes that their members feel hold a mirror up to reality—though it be a fun-house mirror. Then to tell members of a group that their stereotypical image of an outsider is unrealistic is to say something pointless or meaningless; even if they profess beliefs to please you, they will not really abandon the stereotype that so well suits their thinking. So our task is to go behind the female stereotype to see why it has the form it does.

I have already discussed the distinction between real and conventional use of strategies. It is possible to be truly deferential, to really have as one's main concern what the other person wants, and to really have one's own choice of what to think or do depend on the other's—and equally possible to be conventionally so, as when someone knows perfectly well whether, for instance, he (or she) wishes to go to the opera (or bowling) and says meekly, "It's up to you, dear." The same duality of interpretation exists in the enforcement of the other strategies as well: the politician's apparent Clarity, the diplomat's Distance, the salesman's Camaraderie—all are conventional. And indeed, conventional application of all these rules is found to a less pronounced degree in all our behavior. We need not sneer or protest our total sincerity: were it not for conventional politeness and our willingness to use it and interpret it kindly, civilization would likely dissolve in no time at all.[5]

But conventional application of a strategy occurs only in case that strategy is seen as the target for an individual in a particular cultural context. For the Japanese, male and female, conventional Deference is common, where for the German it is not. For the traditional American male, Distance/Clarity has been the target, and so we find in this group's behavior much conventional Distance and Clarity. But Deference is not targeted, and is not conventionally expected, of a male in this culture. And even when overt Deference occurs, we still do not find the extra-linguistic indicators of Deference in the behavior of a normal American man—e.g. downcast eyes, giggle, an attitude of general helplessness—although we do find such behavior among Japanese males, as we might expect. We might interpret this discrepancy as showing that the extralinguistic devices are the most apt to be used, and interpreted, as conventional. So these are good

---

[5] The same point is made about the social utility of disclaimers of action (e.g., the same sorts of hedges and indirections discussed here) by Roy Schafer in his *A New Language for Psychoanalysis* (1976), Yale University Press, New Haven and London.

tests of the targeted politeness for a group—what indirect, and therefore perhaps not entirely conscious or intentional, indicators of a strategy are employed.

Now if a strategy is the target for a particular group, a member of that group will know that behavior in accordance with that strategy may be interpretable either as real, or as conventional. But for nontarget strategies, only real behavior can be inferred. And although one might think that people might learn that other groups make different strategies their targets and so apply them conventionally, people generally seem to be unable to transcend their own systems: participants can interpret others' strategies conventionally only in case they themselves could use them conventionally (because their group makes them targets). People who retain perspective and flexibility in interpretation better than others are felt to have special understanding of groups and cultures other than their own, but they are admired as the exception rather than the rule.

American women's traditional target is Deference as men's is Distance/Clarity. So we find certain kinds of conventional behavior based on these strategies in women's behavior, which men do not normally adopt. This is the reason why men are in general unable to interpret feminine behavior as conventional, rather than real, and hence regularly misinterpret women's intentions. And then, when women respond to their misapprehensions by acting, apparently, unpredictably this gives rise to the stereotype of women as fickle, deceitful and untrustworthy, and illogical—all valid perceptions from the standpoint of male-centered strategies. Since, however, these are tacitly or explicitly recognized as *the* strategies, women themselves have often, shamefacedly or gleefully, gone along with the implied definition of womanhood as perversity. This view is neatly summarized by the male cry of consternation: What do women want?

The reader might object that what is said here about men's inability to accurately interpret women's style must surely have a parallel in women's inability to interpret men's style. To a limited extent this parallelism indeed exists: It is unlikely that women understand men much better than men understand women. But there the similarity ends. For women do not make the assumption that their ways are the healthy and good ones, or the only ones. So women do not, on the basis of their misunderstanding, construct stereotypes of men as irrational, untrustworthy, or silly; they merely assume that men's behavior is beyond their poor comprehension. Thus, women's inability to understand men does not cause them to derogate men, as men's inability causes men and women both to form unfavorable stereotypes of women. Although in reality the inability of men and women to interpret each other's style is totally parallel, because men's style is defined as the norm, only women's is interpreted as aberrant and only women's is subject to stereotyping and being considered as a curiosity worthy of study.

If the American male's conventionalized style is best distinguished as Distancing, how are we to describe styles that seem to belong even further to this strategy? For example, to the American, the typical German—male or female—seems stereotypically aloof and unemotional, not to say arrogant and brusque. Is this not quintessential Distance? Yet to the American, the German stereotype seems light-years away from his.

This is, I think, but a seeming contradiction. It does illustrate the conceptual difficulty inherent in thinking of style as a two-dimensional continuum. For there are various aspects of behavior intertwining here, which we must sort out if we are to resolve the difficulty.

The styles of two different cultures may differ from each other for any of several reasons within this framework. The cases already discussed are those in which the targets themselves differ: women prefer Deference, men Distance. But styles can be differentiated in other ways. Within a group, participants adhere to the idealized target up till a certain point in a relationship. Then, more or less implicitly, they may drop the conventionalization and behave toward one another as they "really" feel. Some cultures have explicit institutionalized means of effecting this switch: Germans, for instance, have a ceremony called *Bruderschaft,* in which the participant of higher status invites a more lowly acquaintance of long standing to use *du* rather than *Sie* as the term of address. With this use of the familiar pronoun go other marks of familiarity—first-naming among them. In American society, first-naming is normal for most relationships within a very short period of acquaintance, and between persons of very different statuses. The implication is that in American society, Distance is the normal and conventionalized strategy only under some circumstances—very early indeed in a relationship, and an impersonal relationship at that. Camaraderie takes over quite early in a friendship for most people. So it might be that American Distance is just as distant as its Germanic equivalent, but shows up in fewer kinds of relationships because Americans drop the convention earlier.

Another interpretation of the difference might be that, in fact, the mixture is different, or that two or more strategies are conventionalized in one culture, corresponding to one in the other. The range of situations covered in Germanic culture by Distance alone is partially covered, for the American man, by Distance, partially by conventionalized Camaraderie. The superficial result of either of these two hypotheses would be the same: to the casual observer, in many circumstances the American would appear to be open and sociable when his German equivalent would appear aloof. But the first theory says this is true because the American becomes truly friendlier faster, the second because he adopts conventional friendly behavior where the German does not have this option.

Finally, differences can arise because what one culture classifies as appropriate Distance behavior, another may consider suitable for Camaraderie, or, more likely, Deference or Clarity. Refusing a second helping of food may, for one group, be a form of conventional Deference: it means that the other person now can take charge, do the urging; the eater will not express his or her own desires. In this case, the expectation will be that, upon urging, the second helping will be accepted, perhaps with a show of reluctance. But refusing seconds may also be seen as Distancing, real or conventional—a refusal to show pleasure, to react to the feeder's attempts at interaction through food. To refuse a second helping is tantamount to saying, "I don't want anything from you. Don't bother me." Of course, if the feeder is following the first pattern and the eater the second, or vice versa, bewilderment and outright anger are apt to ensue.

The contrast between the German and the American male seems best described by the second of these three possibilities. Americans appear to use a split strategy where Germans use a unified one. This difference may occur because there is motion in the American culture where there is none, or a much less perceptible one, in the German. There would seem to be some interesting evidence for this position.

In the last generation or so, the target for American men has been subtly shifting from Distance/Clarity, still prevalent in older people and people raised in traditional milieux, to Camaraderie, which is the preferred mode of presentation of self in younger people. It is probably true that this change originated in the West and is spreading East, with California as usual at the forefront: normal male behavior in California seems very informal and at least superficially intimate, compared with Eastern mores; there is a quicker transition to first names and nicknames, people seem more ready to discuss intimate facts of their lives, and there is a good deal more touching and feeling not only countenanced among men, but indeed expected. This is fast becoming the conventionalized target everywhere.[6] Just as Distance-related behavior was conventional when it was the target, so Camaraderie is conventionalized. The new intimacies are really no more intimate than the old uninvolvements were truly uninvolved.

If this is indeed the case, we have another argument for assuming that stylistic behavior is rule-governed and analogous to a linguistic grammar. Just like the latter, its rules change; or, more accurately, what happens in both cases is that the context, the environment, in which a rule is applicable,changes with time. Camaraderie *used* to be applicable only in relationships of comfort and long standing, in which case, not being a target, it was real: when someone called you by your first name, you knew you were at an intimate stage in your relationship. While this is still marginally normal behavior in the East (or so I am told), the use of title-last name is obsolescent in the Bay Area in almost *any* relationship. It is becoming common, for instance, for doctors to insist on *mutual* first-name address with their patients, and the use of mutual first-name is, I am told, almost *de rigueur* among psychotherapists where I live, although I am similarly told that it is much less obligatory in the East. Obviously, this kind of camaraderie *is* pure convention since there is no mutuality or intimacy elsewhere in the relationship.[7]

---

[6] Cf. the essay in *Time* magazine of July 11, 1977: "A Nation Without Last Names," by Lance Morrow (p. 43).

[7] Actually, the decision as to whether patient and therapist are to reciprocally use first names or title-last names may have more to do with the type of therapy than its geographical locale, with psychoanalytically-oriented types tending toward the latter and human potential or radical psychiatry practice toward the former. However, the point remains valid as the psychotherapeutic method of choice seems closely related to geographical region as indicated, undoubtedly by no coincidence.

Just as the rules of the linguistic grammar change over time, back and forth, but are perpetually in flux, so there is some interesting evidence that these Rapport rules have changed over time: this is not the first time that we have switched our targets. This is an important point, since one might otherwise think that the shift from Clarity/Distance to Camaraderie was an unprecedented step in human behavior, induced by the media, greater mobility, and so forth. It is undoubtedly true that it is harder to live comfortably in an era where the rules are in flux, as is the case in this society at present, than in a relatively stable order—say, Victorian Europe. But our present situation is by no means unique; indeed, just like the linguistic grammar, stylistic grammar *must* shift and always is partially in flux, although the changes are seldom evident to a contemporary member of the culture.

There is an interesting illustration of an earlier period of rule-change in Philippe Ariès's book (1962). Although Ariès does not address the issue directly, much of what he talks about can be interpreted in terms of Rapport rules and change in target. During the thirteenth century various stylistic modalities were in flux in Europe. People were beginning to develop a notion of privacy: they began building houses with separate rooms, wearing more constraining and concealing clothing. About this time too, I believe, last names were being devised and used. All of these work toward a Distancing form of rapport. So we can infer from this sort of evidence that European society during this era was shifting from a target of Camaraderie to one of Distance. We would expect in such a period of flux to find more discomfort than usual among people as they realized their old internalized rule-systems were inappropriate but did not know yet what was expected of them in the new. And so it is not surprising to find in Ariès a discussion of the vogue of etiquette books, in the form of so-called "courtesy manuals," in this historical period. Courtesy manuals played a crucial part in the medieval educational system, and these etiquette books, judging from Ariès's excerpts, are designed to teach Distancing behavior: they contain rules like "Don't touch yourself in public, nor other people"; "don't be too familiar in address"; "dress modestly"; "don't tell your dreams to people." The aim is to appear as unobtrusive and unintrusive as possible—clearly, the establishment of conventions of Distance.

It is true that similar Distancing etiquette manuals have remained around up till the present, but seldom have they been accorded the importance that they were during this period. There will always be some residual insecurity about the correct formulas for achieving the idealized and conventional mode of rapport, but never so much as when the targets themselves are shifting.

Then if it is true that we are now in just such a state of flux, we should expect to find a similar desperate emphasis on etiquette manuals. If we think only of Emily Post-type etiquette, we shall be disappointed: no one seems terribly concerned with the right oyster fork any more. But indeed we *do* have a veritable outpouring of Camaraderie advice in books, magazine and newspaper columns, TV and radio talk shows, and so on: the contemporary analog of the medieval etiquette manual is the psychological self-help book. All of these "manuals" have to do with becoming a good human being in a Camaraderie strategy. No longer are we concerned with being unobtrusive and uninvolved. Rather, our present-day etiquette rules offer injunctions about how to be assertive but not aggressive, how to show you care, how to show you like others and how to be liked—all Camaraderie behavior. So our present situation is parallel to the one in effect several hundred years ago, only in reverse. At that time the target was going from Camaraderie to Distance; now it is going in the opposite direction. But our behavior in the midst of such a change is apparently not significantly different from that of our forebears: we feel insecure and look to authorities to instruct us in the new propriety.

An enlightening sidelight, relevant to the larger issue of this paper, has to do with who writes the etiquette manuals; who are the social arbiters. In the earlier period of flux, the writers of these books as well as their users were men: etiquette was considered crucial enough for men to bother with and take responsibility for. But as it importance waned over the centuries, women became the dominant figures in the world of etiquette: just as with other concerns that are deemed by a society to be peripheral to survival, like fashion and grammar, manners gradually came to be a feminine province so that, most recently, virtually all the arbiters of correct deportment have been women. Interestingly, the trend is now reversed. As the new etiquette is felt to be important and necessary to one's survival, it has become the province of men at least as much as of women: men are no longer ashamed to be reading and writing instructions for proper human behavior. Here again we have evidence that we are in a period of flux, because the learning of the new system is considered important enough to be the business of men.

Earlier in this paper I correlated the use of Clarity/Distance with obsessive-compulsive symptomatology, noting (as has been frequently pointed out) that this form of neurotic behavior has been common among men in our society, just as hysterical character correlated with Deference and Camaraderie, has been prevalent among women. More recently, within the last generation, it has been remarked that these "classical" neuroses—the symptoms on the basis of which psychoanalysis was devised, and for which it is considered particularly effective—have become comparatively uncommon. First in their symptomatic and more recently in their characterological forms, they have lost ground as presenting symptoms. Psychotherapists are seeing more of so-called "narcissistic characters." (In this connection, there is a most interesting article by Christopher Lasch, 1976.) Just as the obsessional neurotic's form of rapport is an exaggerated Distance and Clarity, and the hysteric's, Deference (which manifests itself in seductiveness and the fuzziness of attention discussed by Shapiro), the narcissistic person's is conventional Camaraderie. Since narcissism, as discussed by psychoanalytically-oriented writers, involves an inability to empathize with or form deep relationships with others, we might be inclined to consider it the very opposite of Camaraderie, But in fact superficial friendliness and interest in others—as long as they serve one's purposes—is associated with the narcissistic character, who is desperately concerned with his reception by others and therefore must feign interest in others. Hence, too, the linguistic correlates: nicknames, four-letter words, slang, at least superficial directness. And just as obsessional Clarity is a false clarity, meant to mask perception rather than enhance it, so narcissistic Camaraderie is merely superficial show, and is thus particularly apt to function as conventional behavior. If indeed neurotic symptoms are merely exaggerations of an individual's—or a society's— ideal mode of presentation of self, and it is true that contemporary Americans perceive these traits as desirable, in contradistinction to those of Distance and Deference, this fact merely provides evidence for our targeting of Camaraderie. For if all this camaraderie has become the new target of rapport, then it all fits together perfectly; narcissism is the obvious choice of neurosis for a Camaraderie-based culture.

If we accept this idea that society is becoming Camaraderie-oriented, there is still one question to be answered: we have been evading the issue of *whose* system is changing. It is clear that the male stereotype of Clarity/Distance is yielding to Camaraderie; but what is happening with women? I said earlier that one thing that makes it particularly hard to be female in this culture at this time is the fact that one cannot be a good woman (using Deference/Camaraderie) and a good human being (defined, androcentrically, in terms of Clarity/Distance) at once. What then is happening to women's style here at this time, and if there is a change, what does it augur?

There are several possibilities. First, women's style may be coming closer to pure Camaraderie as men's becomes so too. In this case our culture would end up looking in a curious way analogous to that of contemporary Japan. For the Japanese, Deference is the target for both sexes—but a different sort of Deference, and under more conditions, for women. Although the requirement for exaggerated Deference still makes women subservient to men, nonetheless it may allow the Japanese woman to experience fewer confusions in defining her ideal role: it may well be possible in Japanese culture, as it is not in ours, to be an ideal woman *and* an ideal human being at once, without paradox. As another alternative women's style may stay the same, with men's moving around it; and a third, while men's style shifts in one direction, women's might shift in another—to Distance, or Clarity, for instance. In the third case, we might expect to find in time that Clarity was no longer viewed as the embodiment of all that is rational and human; and women, having tried to gain acceptance as human beings by adopting the "healthy human being" behavior would find themselves once again on the losing end of the stick, since ideal human behavior would still be defined in terms of men's behavior. If the second option is the one that is occurring, we might expect no significant change in women's image and perception of themselves. If in fact both sexes are changing to be more alike, then we may have a chance to see real changes in the way women are regarded and regard themselves. Ideally, the members of a society should allow for pluralism and flexibility in style, should be able to realize that various modes of presentation of self may be appropriate, and none by itself defines a human being. But, realistically, this is not apt to happen, and we can only hope for change in women's image as women become more like men, in this case both changing to a new mode of behavior.

What evidence exists in media representations suggests that the first option is winning out, and I think it is the healthiest possible choice. Just as women are becoming freer in the extent and types of self-expression open to them, so—perhaps more slowly—are men. Showing care and concern, crying, and expressing a wide range of emotion have not been characteristic of men's style, as they are the antithesis of Clarity/Distance. By the same token, wearing severe man-tailored suits and having the latest stock market quotations at one's fingertips have not been permissible for women as users of Deference/Camaraderie. But both are becoming common, despite the denunciations and expressions of apocalypse that issue from the conservative press. We shall have to be patient and await the final outcome of the stylistic reorganization that we see occurring around us, just as our forebears had to wait many centuries to see the final result of the change initiated during the medieval period.

To say that style is changing for all of us implies a grammar of style that we unconsciously utilize; to say that men's and women's styles are becoming more similar is to make a less theoretical point, but one of great significance for our future as men, women, and people. In any event, what we observe about the times in which we are living can tell us a great deal both about human psychological capacities and about what we are striving to become.

ACKNOWLEDGMENTS

The preparation of this paper has profited from my discussion of its contents with many people, as well as numerous opportunities to present its ideas in various stages, to many groups. In particular I would like to thank Linda Coleman for her very helpful suggestions leading to the final form of the stylistic continuum as it appears here; and Deborah Tannen for innumerable valuable improvements in both style and content.

REFERENCES

ARIÈS, P. 1962. Centuries of Childhood. Knopf, New York.
BROVERMAN, I.K. et al. 1970. Sex-role stereotypes and clinical judgements of mental health. Journal of Consulting and Clinical Psychology 34:1, 1-7.
CHOMSKY, N. 1965. Aspects of the Theory of Syntax. The M.I.T. Press. Cambridge, Mass.
— 1968. Language and Mind. Harcourt, Brace & World. New York.

GRICE, H.P. 1975. Logic and conversation. *In* Syntax and Semantics 3: Speech Acts. P. Cole & J.L. Morgan, Eds. Academic Press. New York.

LAKOFF, R. 1975. Language and Woman's Place. Harper & Row. New York.

— 1976. Why you can't say what you mean: a review of Strictly Speaking, by Edwin Newman. Centrum **IV:2.**151-170.

— 1977. Woman's language as paradigm in a grammar of style. Language and Style, December, 1977.

LASCH, C. 1976. The Narcissist Society. The New York Review of Books, September 30, 1976.

SHAPIRO, D. 1965. Neurotic Styles. Basic Books. New York.

Abstract

AGAINST OUR WILL: MALE INTERRUPTIONS OF FEMALES IN CROSS-SEX CONVERSATION

Candace West

It has been suggested that women "ask for" the discriminatory treatment they frequently receive from men in a variety of situations. In a previous study of naturally occurring conversations West observed that men interrupt women more often than women interrupt men or than either sex interrupts in same-sex conversations. West's concern was with "deep" interuptions, those that occur "more than two syllables away from a terminal boundary of a possibly complete utterance," and that are not confirmations of what the speaker is saying, such as the interjection, "Yeah." Deep intrusions may be considered attempts to take control of the conversation.

In the present study West analyzed responses to deep intrusions by male and female speakers in cross-sex conversations among previously unacquainted college students. Specifically, she wanted to determine whether females were more submissive than males in coping with interruptions, thereby contributing to the liklihood of being further interrupted. A hierarchy of responses varying from submissiveness to assertiveness was developed.

Males were found to interrupt females three times as often as females interrupted males, confirming West's earlier observation. However, females were as likely as males to respond assertively to interruptions. These results do not generate displays of "submission" by females.

Editors

AGAINST OUR WILL: MALE INTERRUPTIONS OF FEMALES IN CROSS-SEX CONVERSATION*

Candace West

*Department of Sociology
Florida State University
Tallahassee, Florida 32306*

INTRODUCTION

A disturbing suggestion is sometimes made to the effect that women "ask for" discriminatory and even brutal treatment by men. In lay communities, the most blatant form of this suggestion (i.e., women invite rape) is increasingly deplored.[1] However, when they are made in the context of empirical inquiry, suggestions with similar implications may go overlooked. In discussions of the initiation of simultaneous talk (cf. Zimmerman and West, 1975; West and Zimmerman, 1977) reports of males' systematic interruptions of females often draw questions regarding women's part in creating, sustaining or inviting men's interruptions of their utterances. For example, I have observed females falling silent for longer and longer durations after repeated interruptions by males (Zimmerman and West, 1975: 117-124). One interpretation of this observation is that females engage in a form of silent protest against male intrusion into their turns. Another explanation I have heard offered for this finding is that females' silence "encourages" males' interruption. In fact, the topics women talk about, the "style" of "women's talk," and the extent to which they protest when men violate their conversational turnspace have all been offered as reasons for males' interruptions of females. Male dominance in conversation might be likened to our cultural (and sometimes legal) conceptions of rape. Women are seen by some to invite rape by the clothes they wear, the "style" of "women's walk" and, especially, for their failure to "put up a fight."[2] However, the extent to which we find empirical bases for the existence of a struggle is the extent to which dominance in conversation and physical rape may both be defined as conflict situations and not willing submission.

* (With thanks to Susan Brownmiller.) This paper is based in part on the author's doctoral dissertation, *Communicating Gender: A Study of Dominance and Control in Conversation,* Department of Sociology, University of California, Santa Barbara, 1978. She thanks Don H. Zimmerman, James D. Orcutt, Marilyn Lester, Sarah Fenstermaker Berk, Nancy Meyers Blumberg, and the reviewers of this journal for their helpful comments on earlier versions.

[1] An example is provided by the case of the Madison, Wisconsin trial judge who was recalled by his constituency after "remarks from the bench linking rape to provocative women's clothing" (The New York Times, September 9, 1977: B1).

[2] See Henley (1977), particularly Chapter 1: "The walk, like the clothing, is taken as a sign of sexual invitation that overrules one's words or other action." (p. 1).

81

0077-8923/0327-0081 $01.75/2 ©1979, NYAS

Elsewhere (Zimmerman and West, 1975; West and Zimmerman, 1977), I report findings of a study of 20 same-sex and 11 cross-sex exchanges between pairs of college-age adults recorded in various natural settings within a college community, and five parent-child exchanges recorded in a physician's office. Results of that investigation suggested that females and children receive similar treatment in conversations with males and parents respectively: both women and children were much more frequently interrupted by their conversational partners.

Here, I report findings on a collection of cross-sex conversations between previously unaquainted persons recorded under controlled conditions, which bear upon the reproducibility of my earlier findings. Further, I extend my analysis of the initiation of interruptions to consider how speakers negotiate who shall drop out and who shall continue when these intrusions occur. My results indicate that females, in conversations with unacquainted males, do not appear to "invite" the males' interruption of their utterances through any female failure to compete for a turnspace or retrieve their interrupted utterances. And yet, males interrupt females far more often than the reverse, even in brief conversations in a laboratory setting.

Since the central concern of this paper is the negotiation of simultaneous turns at talk, I begin with a description of conversational turn-taking (Sacks, Schegloff, and Jefferson, 1974) and a series of observations on orderly procedures for resolving and retrieving simultaneous utterances (Jefferson and Schegloff, 1975).

NEGOTIATING SIMULTANEOUS SPEECH

Sacks *et al.* (1974) suggest that conversations are organized to ensure that (1) one party speaks at a time and (2) speaker change recurs. These features describe a normative order of interaction (i.e., the preferred order from the viewpoint of conversationalists.) Therefore, given the onset of two or more speakers talking at once, the most immediate problem they are faced with is the resolution of that state of simultaneity.

My earlier work (Zimmerman and West, 1975; West and Zimmerman, 1977) distinguishes between two types of simultaneous speech: overlaps (briefly, errors in transition-timing) and interruptions (violations of speaker turns). Here, I am interested in deep interruptions, which are defined as instances of simultaneous speech that involve deep intrustions into the internal structure of speakers' utterances. By "deep," I mean more than two syllables away from the terminal boundaries of a possibly complete utterance (a word, phrase, clause or sentence depending on its context.) This definition is based on Sacks *et al.*'s suggestion that a turn consists not only of the temporal duration of an utterance but of the right and obligation to speak which is allocated to a current speaker. Turns are constructed of what they term "unit-types," which can consist of words, phrases, clauses or sentences depending on their context. Each speaker, upon being allocated a turn, is provided the "right" to complete at least one unit-type before turn-transition ought properly to occur. (See Sacks *et al.,* 1974; and Zimmerman and West, 1975 for more detailed discussion of the turn-taking model.)

To be sure, there are instances of simultaneous speech that appear to ratify—rather than disrupt—the talk of a current speaker, e.g., the emphatic "YEAH" interjected to display recognition of that which is in-the-course-of-being-said (Jefferson, 1973). Deep interruptions, on the other hand, cannot be seen to be "warranted" by such considerations of active listenership. Instead, this type of simultaneous speech is seen to disrupt turns at talk, disorganize the ongoing construction of conversational topics; and violate the current speaker's right to be engaged in speaking (cf. West and Zimmerman, 1977). The following example provides an illustration of its effect. (The transcribing conventions employed here appear in the AP-PENDIX to this paper. In this example, the brackets enclosing the female's and male's utterances indicate those portions of talk which are simultaneous.)

(Excerpt from Zimmerman and West corpus, 1975)
    Male: Where the hell have *you* been?
(1.4)
    Female: Well I had to find Foster n'⌈then⌉
    Male: ⌊Do ⌋you realize
        what time it is?
(2.0)
    Female: Uh *yeah* but I couldn't find ⌈Fos⌉
    Male: ⌊I've⌋ been *standing around* in that cruddy reserve
        bookroom for the last half hour!
    (#)
    Female: Sshush! the whole hall is gonna hear ⌈you⌉
    Male: ⌊I ⌋   don't care! Next time you wanna
        "just stop off on campus" you can use your legs!

In this example, the male who is inquiring as to the prior whereabouts of the (evidently late) female does not appear to be seriously interested in listening to her answer. Repeatedly, he interrupts her attempts to explain, even by posing a further question ("Do you know what time it is?") *over* her ongoing answer to his initial inquiry ("Where the hell have *you* been?"). Note that the female resolves the state of simultaneity produced by his first incursion by dropping out midsentence (". . .'n then".) Dropping out could indeed be seen as tantamount to "not putting up a fight" in this context, since the turnspace is ceded to the interrupting party (cf. Jefferson and Schegloff, 1975).[3] However, note too that the female *reintroduces* her objection-thus-

---

[3] See Jefferson and Schegloff, 1975, for the detailed discussion of these procedures and their structural significance for conversation. Here, purposes at hand prohibit more than a general overview of the interactional consequences of resolution and retrieval types.

far in her very next turn (" . . . *yeah* but I couldn't find Fos"). While her recycling of the explanation can hardly be seen to confront his prior intrusion head on, it does suggest that more than "passive surrender" is involved here.

Jefferson and Schegloff (1975) specify a variety of procedures employed by speakers to resolve a state of overlap and restore talk to a state of one-party-at-a-time.[4] One method, of course, is dropping out to cede the turn-space to the other. But any given speaker in a particular state of simultaneity might not exercise the option of dropping out and instead persevere by continuing the construction of an utterance—waiting, perhaps, for the other speaker(s) to drop out. Or, a speaker might struggle for conversational space by progressively getting louder over the talk of a co-conversationalist:

(Excerpt from West and Zimmerman corpus, 1978)

> *Male* 1: There was no things like tow::els ⌈'r anything like that.⌉
> *Male* 2:   ⟶ ⌊We:ll TOW: ⌋ els er go:od, but the
> sheets are scREWed cuz ther're not fi:dded sheets y'know?

Jefferson and Schegloff (1975) also suggest that a speaker might even engage in an active fight for the floor by recycling portions of a speech object over the talk of another, in order to project the rest of that utterance in the clear:

(Excerpt from West and Zimmerman corpus, 1978)

> *Male* 1: Yeah, for sure, I gu:ess. Y'know ⌈I don't   ⌉ ↙
> *Male* 2:   ⌊Of the- in the⌋ in the top of the atmosphere

In the above examples, we see speakers manipulating the sounds and structures of their utterances within a state of simultaneity, and resuming "normal" pronounciation in the clear. In the first excerpt, "Male 1" proceeds to completion of his utterance, then yields to "Male 2's" progressively louder claims for the floor. "Finishing" within a state of simultaneous speech is, in my view, yet another distinct means of resolving it. While this procedure cedes the turnspace to another, it virtually denies that the incursion was disruptive by leaving a completed utterance in its wake. In contrast, the speaker who drops midsentence leaves "unfinished business" behind.

---

[4] The distinction between overlap and interruption is made by Zimmerman and me. Jefferson, Sacks and Schegloff refer to all instances of simultaneity as "overlapping" utterances. Hence, when I talk about a "state of overlap." I am using the word generically to include all instances of simultaneity.

Of course, for speakers who finish in overlap, (see the excerpt just above) and certainly for those who drop out, there is a danger that their utterances will turn out to have been "lost" following the resolution of that simultaneity. As Jefferson and Schegloff note, overlap may itself obscure hearing and/or understanding simultaneous utterances (e.g., it is difficult to make out what someone is saying while you are in the process of talking over them). Moreover, since turn-transition is accomplished on a turn-by-turn basis (Sacks *et al.,* 1974), the relevant sequential basis for a "next" turn or next topic may be unclear in the event of simultaneous last utterances.[5]

Jefferson and Schegloff (1975) observe a variety of retrieval procedures that are used to deal with the possible sequencing and intelligibility problems posed by simultaneous speech. Speakers may, for example, retrieve by restarting their *own* overlapped utterances, as the female did her attempts at explanation in the excerpt dealing with her tardiness. A speaker might, on the other hand, retrieve portions of a *co-conversationalist's* overlapped utterance, e.g., through requesting that it be repeated:

(Excerpt from corpus reported here)

> *Female:* Hm:m (#) Maybe the bELL's not gonna ring-henh-henh-henh-henh-henh .hh!
>   hunh- ⌈heh .hh .hh-.hh   ⌉
> *Male:*   ⌊I think they're wai⌋ tin' for us to finish. Before they're gonna ring
>   it.
> →*Female:* Hm:m?
> *Male:* ((yawning)) I think they're WAITing for us to finish before they're gonna ring it.

Other-retrieval may also be effected through incorporating portions of the other's overlapped talk in ones own next utterance:

(Excerpt from corpus reported here)

> *Female:* So, 'r you taking Che:m?
> *Male:* Oh: yeah. Chem One Ay. Math Three Ay. U:h Physics.
> *Female:* Which one? (x) ⌈Are ⌉   you taki- Uh: .h Eight's sposed
> *Male:*   ⌊Eight⌋
> *Female:* to be (harder) 'n six.

---

[5] For example, the answer to a question is only intelligible as such given that a question has been audibly posed in the first instance. And consider further the situation of someone who is asked to respond to two different questions which are posed simultaneously. Which question requires "first" answer?

In both examples, the female ensures that the male's overlapped talk will not be lost in subsequent conversation, either by asking him to repeat it or by incorporating some portion of it in her own next utterance to indicate that he has been heard and understood.

Clearly then, the negotiation of simultaneous speech is an intricate process, entailing considerable interactional work on the part of conversationalists. While the model of conversational turn-taking advanced by Sacks et al. (1974) provides a theoretical basis establishing speakers' rights to speak, Jefferson and Schegloff's (1975) observations are employed below in a preliminary examination of speakers' methods of preserving, protecting and defending those rights in cross-sex conversations.

METHODS

The five two-party conversations analyzed in this paper were recorded in a laboratory setting. Conversationalists were university students (5 females and 5 males) who were recruited from introductory sociology classes to participate in "a study of face-to-face interaction." All participants were white, single college-age adults.[6] They were randomly paired with partners of the other sex with whom they were previously unacquainted, in order to maximize the possibility that politeness rules (e.g., "don't interrupt") would be observed. Conversations were produced by the suggestion that participants "relax and get to know one another" prior to their discussion of a problem specified by the researcher (bicycle safety on campus). Each exchange so produced lasted a total of 12 minutes. The resulting audiotapes yielded 107 pages of transcribed conversation, in which initiations, resolutions and retrievals of interruption were classified using the coding procedures outlined below.[7]

Deep interruptions, as defined earlier, are instances of simultaneous speech which are initiated well within the internal structure of a current speaker's utterance—violating that speaker's rights to the turnspace. Operationally, classification of deep interruptions relied on two criteria: (1) identifying instances of simultaneity which were initiated more than two syllables away from the terminal boundaries of a possibly complete utterance (i.e., a word, phrase, clause or sentence) and (2) of these, coding only those instances which appeared to disrupt a current speaker's turn at talk.[8]

---

[6] Volunteers under eighteen and over twenty-one years of age were excluded from participation, in order to obtain partners of roughly the same age group. However, neither race nor ethnic background were solicited on the initial volunteer forms. Therefore, some participants appeared for scheduled sessions that were conducted, but their talk was not included in the data base for analysis.

[7] To minimize the transcriber's difficulty in deciphering two parties at once, participants wore lavaliere microphones and were recorded in stereo. Under circumstances of ambiguity, (e.g., when sounds were heard that were capable of more than one interpretation), these ambiguities are indicated in the transcripts themselves. (See APPENDIX).

[8] As noted above, deep intrusions into the structure of a current speaker's turn need not necessarily disrupt that turn. For example, "saying the same thing at the same time" may serve

The alternative methods of negotiation suggested by Jefferson and Schegloff's (1975) observations were collapsed into the more general categories shown in FIGURE 1.

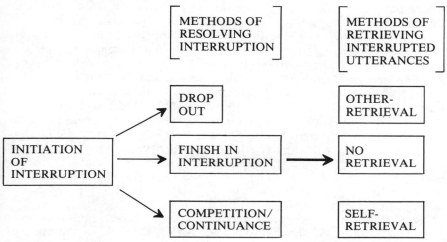

FIGURE 1. Negotiation of deep interruptions (hierarchically arrayed by extent to which current speakers assert their rights to speak).

Both resolutions and retrivals of interruptions are hierarchically arrayed in order of the extent to which speakers assert their conversational rights (with the "least assertive" categories at the top). For example, the most assertive method of resolving a deep interruption is "competition/continuance." This category includes those procedures that insist on ones *own* rights to a turnspace; getting louder, stuttering, stretching or recycling portions of ones talk over another's ongoing utterance. "Continuance" is also included in this category, since the speaker employing it perseveres in claiming the turn for him or herself over the other's simultaneous speech. A less assertive and less obtrusive means of resolving interruption is "finishing": completing the interrupted utterance within a state of simultaneity. This method, as noted above, cedes the turnspace to the other, but leaves an intact unit-type behind. "Dropping out" is the least assertive form of resolution provided by the scheme: abrupt termination of ones own utterance midway into production (Jefferson and Schegloff, 1975).

However, dropping out need not turn out to have been a "passive surrender" of ones talk or ones turnspace, depending on what (if any) form of retrieval is employed in its wake. Retrievals are, by definition, retroactive procedures that repair or reinstate overlapping utterances after the fact. The

---

to ratify—rather than disorganize—the utterance being produced by a current speaker (Jefferson, 1973).

most assertive form of retrieval included in the scheme for a recipient of interruption is "self-retrieval": continuing from where one dropped, or
restarting ones utterance anew after having dropped to restore talk to a state
of one-party-at-a-time. Thus, the speaker who drops to resolve an interruption and subsequently engages in self-retrieval is (albeit belatedly) standing
up for his or her rights to have been speaking before the drop occurred. But
the speaker employing "other-retrieval"—by acknowledging, requesting a
repetition or embedding portions of another's simultaneous talk in his or
her own next utterance—retroactively cedes the simultaneous turn to the
other. Moreover, one who drops to resolve a state of simultaneity and then
other-retrieves further ratifies the other party's prior rights to that conversational space. By way of analogy, we might view other-retrievals in much
the same way as Goffman (1967; p.56) does "deference rituals", i.e., "as a
symbolic means by which appreciation is . . . conveyed *to* a recipient *of* this
recipient." In this context, appreciation consists of the retroactive
acknowledgment of the other's conversational rights by repairing her or his
previously overlapped utterance, and by placing it in "first" position for
subsequent remarks.

Retrieval of ones own or another's utterance is not guaranteed for any
particular instance of simultaneous speech. So, included in the coding
scheme is the general category of "nonretrieval," i.e., the absence of those
procedures identified by Jefferson and Schegloff (1975) in places where they
might have been employed following the resolution of simultaneous talk.
The absence of retrieval is noticeable since it, in effect, denies the need for
repair or restoration of *either* party's overlapping utterance. Also included
in coding is the possibility that more than one form of resolution (e.g., getting louder while recycling) and more than one form of retrieval (e.g.,
acknowledging and repeating) might accompany any given instance of
simultaneity. Since Jefferson and Schegloff's (1975) observations only provide preliminary indications of restrictions on resolution-retrieval combinations, the scheme permits identification of multiple resolutions and
retrievals by either or both speakers. I turn now to consider the distributions
of these procedures in the cross-sex conversations that make up my collection.[9]

FINDINGS

My earlier study of cross-sex and same-sex exchanges utilized data
recorded in "natural settings," e.g., drug stores, coffee shops, and other
public places in a university community (Zimmerman and West, 1975).

---

[9] Of course, this collection does not constitute a probability sample, so it would be inappropriate to use the usual logic of statistical inference in generalizing from these findings to
conversation or conversationalist at large. My purpose, however, is not generalization but
specification of a method of examining conflict and competition in conversation as empirical
questions in their own right, using Jefferson and Schegloff's (1975) observations.

Results found interruptions were distributed nearly equally between 20 same-sex conversational partners. Cross-sex exchanges, in contrast, displayed marked asymmetries: males interrupted females far more often than the reverse, initiating 96 percent of all interruptions that occurred.

Here I find cross-sex conversations recorded in a laboratory setting also display asymmetries, though not in such dramatic patterns. A total of 28 deep interruptions were observed, of which 21 or 75 percent were initiated by males.[10] TABLE 1 presents the proportions of deep interruptions initiated in the exchanges making up this collection: dyads A, B, C, D, and E.

TABLE 1

INITIATION OF DEEP INTERRUPTIONS IN 5 CROSS-SEX CONVERSATIONS

	Male-Initiated	Female-Initiated	Ratio*	Total†
Dyad E‡	4	0	0	4
Dyad A	3	1	3.0	4
Dyad C	5	1	5.0	6
Dyad D	4	2	2.0	6
Dyad B	5	3	1.6	8
	Mean ratio = 2.9			

* Ratios are male/female.

† These figures represent only the incidence of deep interruption in each of the twelve-minute conversations. For the analysis of other types of simultaneous speech which occurred there, see West, 1978.

‡ Dyads are listed in ascending order of total interruptions.

Generally, we find deep interruptions are asymmetrically distributed between partners in these exchanges, even in the two conversations with fewest total numbers of initiations (dyads E and A.) And, in each of these dyads, males interrupt females more often than females interrupt males (4 to 0, 3 to 1, 5 to 1, 4 to 2, and 5 to 3). Moreover, the exchange that is least asymmetrical (or, conversely, most closely approximates equality of distribution) is dyad B—which also contains the largest number of deep interruptions in the collection (8). Thus, these results parallel those found earlier (Zimmerman and West, 1975).

---

[10] For a comparison of these cross-sex exchanges with a collection of same-sex conversations also recorded in this setting see West, 1978 and West and Zimmerman, 1978.

Conversational "Submissiveness": A Methodological Note

A complex yet striking pattern of interrelationship between resolutions and retrievals emerged in the process of coding the instances of deep interruption in these transcripts. Repeatedly, in the course of classifying these events, I noticed that deep interruptions by males were followed by: (1) the male's continuance, and the female's dropping out or finishing within the state of simultaneity; and (2) the male's nonretrieval and the female's nonretrieval or other-retrieval of the male's utterance (which interrupted her in the first instance).

Of all the possible combinations of resolutions and retrievals, these four were observed repeatedly in the transcripts. They are shown in FIGURE 2,

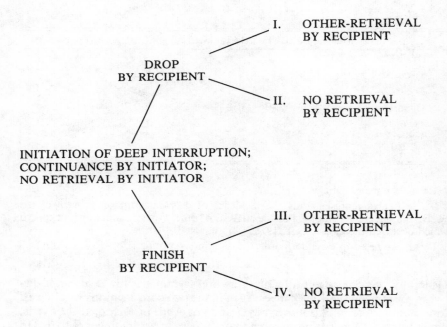

FIGURE 2. Patterns of submission following the initiation of deep interruption.

hierarchically ordered by the extent to which interrupted speakers fail to "put up a fight" when their conversational rights are violated: given the interrupter's intrusion, continuance and nonretrieval, the recipient of interruption (I) drops, to resolve the state of simultaneity and then retrieves the other's interrupting talk; (II) drops, to resolve the state of simultaneity and then does no retrieval; (III) finishes within a state of simultaneity and then other-retrieves; or (IV) finishes within a state of simultaneity and does no retrieval.

Recall my earlier analogy between male dominance in conversation and our cultural conceptions of rape, where both are seen as consequences of females' "invitations" (i.e., their failure to put up a fight). FIGURE 2 reflects a simple, if vulgar, parallel: given that males "dominate" females through deep interruptions of their utterances, do females "ask for it?" That is, do females' responses to males' interruptions approximate a form of invitation to further violations of their turns?

Obviously, all of the alternatives shown in FIGURE 2 are "submissive" to some extent, insofar as none of them entails an active struggle for a turn-space (e.g., competing by getting louder over the talk of another or retrieving ones own utterance by restarting it after being interrupted). That these patterns were observed so frequently is itself notable, given that the model of turn-taking (Sacks *et al.,* 1974) allocates the current turn-holder (i.e., the recipient of interruption) initial rights to the floor.

Of greatest importance however, are comparisons of male and female recipients' use of resolutions and retrievals when interrupted *by one another.* TABLE 2 reports the distribution of resolutions of deep interruptions by sex of recipients. And, as this table show, there are great similarities between male and female recipients' responses to interruption. The most assertive form of resolution, competition/continuance, was rarely employed by females *or* males (14 percent of resolutions in both cases). The less assertive forms of resolution (dropping and finishing within interruption) were employed with roughly equal frequency by *both* sexes (43 versus 38 and 43 versus 48 percent, respectively).

TABLE 2

RESOLUTIONS OF DEEP INTERRUPTIONS IN CROSS-SEX CONVERSATIONS

	Male Recipients %	Female Recipients %
Competition/ continuance	14	14
Finish in interruption	43	38
Drop	43	48
	100 (7)	100 (21)

However, as noted earlier, the use of less assertive forms of resolution need not imply passive surrender, depending on what—if any—form of retrieval is employed in their wake. TABLE 3 displays the distribution of retrievals of interrupted utterances by sex of recipients. As TABLE 3

TABLE 3

RETRIEVALS OF UTTERANCES FOLLOWING DEEP INTERRUPTIONS IN
CROSS-SEX CONVERSATIONS

	Male Recipients %	Female Recipients %
Self-retrieval	14	10
No retrieval	43	71
Other-retrieval	43	19
	100 (7)	100 (21)

indicates, female recipients failed to employ retrievals nearly twice as often as males (71 versus 43 percent). However, male recipients employed other-retrieval (the least assertive response) more than twice as often as females (43 versus 19 percent). And, for the most assertive response (self-retrieval), which might retroactively claim the floor for an interrupted speaker, we see no appreciable difference between male and female recipients (14 versus 10 percent).

In summary then, I find pronounced gender differences in the initiation of interruptions in these conversations. However, types of resolutions employed by recipients of interruption do not differ by gender, nor do types of retrievals that might reassert an interrupted speaker's conversational rights. I move now to consider the implications of these results.

DISCUSSION

Consistent with my earlier findings on cross-sex conversations in natural settings (West and Zimmerman, 1975), results of this study indicate that males interrupt females far more often than the reverse—even in the first minutes of an encounter between strangers in a laboratory setting. However, this finding cannot be explained by females' differential *responses* to interruption. As we have seen, resolutions and retrievals of interrupted utterances generally take "submissive" forms, whether recipients are male or female. The only reason females *appear* to be more submissive is that they are far more frequently interrupted in the first instance.

However, the *fact* that females are in a position to exhibit proportionately more submission than males when conversing with them might just be what gives rise to assertions such as Lakoff's (1975) regarding the greater politeness of woman's speech, or characterizations of it's greater "uncertainty" (cf. McMillan *et al.,* 1977). As Kramer *et al.* (1978) note, it is entirely possible that our stereotypes of male and female personality characteristics are related to "beliefs that the sexes speak in different ways"(p.3). If this is so, it would not be at all surprising if females' exhibition of submissiveness patterns were interpreted as evidence of their "asking for" (or at least, failing to put up a fight against) interruption by males. At this point, I am clearly speculating beyond the findings of this study—since my focus is on actual conversations rather than social perceptions of conversations, I have no way to support these conjectures at this time. However, my data *do* provide a preliminary indication of where one might look for the particulars which could account for stereotypes of "woman's speech"—in those situations in which male dominance (e.g., through repeated and disproportionate interruption of females) is exercised.

Thus, given the fact that males interrupt females more frequently than the reverse in the first instance, speakers engaging in cross-sex conversations may come to orient to those repeated infractions as "more" than independent violations of turnspace and in fact, "more" than isolated violations of speaker's rights to be engaged in speaking: females' resolutions of deep interruption (regardless of "who started it") may themselves come to color the conversational definition of the situation. To sum up with an often quoted but still useful observation, where we ". . . think situations are real, they are real in their consequences" (Thomas, 1931; p. 189). The consequences for women, of course, include the implication that they "get what they ask for."

Conversational Conflict Reconsidered

As noted earlier, the model of conversational turn-taking advanced by Sacks *et al.* (1974) provides the current turn-holder the initial "right" to the floor, at least until a possibly complete utterance is produced. However, both male and female speakers in these transcripts, rather than "insisting" on their rights, show a decided tendency to yield the floor to interrupting parties.[11]

A possible explanation for this finding might be the turn-by-turn organization of conversational sequencing, specified by the model itself (see Sacks *et al.,* 1974). For example, not only turns but topics of talk are seen to

---

[11] Elsewhere (West, 1978; West and Zimmerman, 1978), I find that resolutions and retrievals of other types of simultaneous speech (e.g., overlaps and simultaneous starts) are even less "assertive" than are responses to deep interruption. It appears that my definition of deep interruption is "grounded" in speaker's actual practices: violations of speakers' turnspace more often produce assertive responses from recipients than do errors in transition-timing.

develop on a turn-by-turn basis, such that the relevance of a "next" utterance is contingent on that of a prior utterance. Sacks (1972, n.d.) notes
that complaints regarding interruption (e.g. "Wait," "I wasn't finished
yet," etc.) must be entered in the turns immediately following their occurrence if they are to be effective., Yet voicing a complaint also constitutes
changing the topic of talk at that point. So, speakers interrupted in the
course of developing a topic may be reluctant to complain, since complaints
may themselves further delay or obscure topic development.

Elsewhere (West, 1978), I argue that sustaining a state of simultaneity
(e.g., by competing or continuing) is virtually equivalent to sustaining a
state of confusion over the next turn-transition point, since *which* turn will
form the basis for a next turn becomes increasingly unclear as simultaneous
talk continues. This may pose a dilemma for recipients of interruptions:
whether constraints of turn-allocation (which assign them, as current
speakers, the right to the floor), or those of turn-construction (which require identification of a "prior" turn as the basis for next turn-transition)
shall take priority. Given the focus of Sacks *et al.*'s model is on the *next*
turn and *next* transition, the conversational rights of any particular current
speaker may have less priority (systematically) than the constraints of turn-
transition, other things being equal. In short, concern for the topical and sequential relevance of a "next" turn may override *post facto* disputes over
violations of speakers' rights in the turns just taken.

Speaking interactionally then, concern for preservation of the ongoing
flow of talk *between* persons may supersede occasioned violations of the
rights *of* persons, since the flow itself maintains their identities as co-
participants in a conversation. As Goffman notes:

> The principles of organization of any social system are likely to come in
> conflict at certain points. Instead of permitting the conflict to be expressed
> in an encounter, the individual places himself between the opposing prin-
> ciples. He sacrifices his identity for a moment, and sometimes the en-
> counter, but the principles are preserved. (Goffman, 1967, p.112)

Of course, these conversations were collected under conditions that were expected to maximize observance of politeness rules (e.g., don't interrupt).
Thus, one could argue that overt displays of conflict and competition might
occur under other, more relaxed circumstances. A challenging task for further research is the specification of those conditions under which preservation of the "smooth scene" is subordinated to concern for individual identity.

CONCLUSIONS

The aims of this study were twofold: (1) to determine if the previously
observed pattern of cross-sex interaction (Zimmerman and West, 1975;
West and Zimmerman, 1977) would occur in the initial minutes of a first encounter between strangers in a contrived situation; and (2) to address the
issues of conflict and competition between speakers upon the occurrence of

simultaneity, and the resolution of such states of competitive talk as empirical questions in their own right.

The pattern of male-initiated interruption observed earlier was found here also, but it was not linked to females' failure to "put up a fight." Males and females show similar patterns of response to deep interruption, even though males interrupt females far more often than the reverse.

These findings might serve as a caveat to researchers where investigations of interpersonal power (and, especially, the relationship between gender and leadership) lead to conceptual dichotomies, e.g., measurement and techniques which polarize aggressiveness and passivity or instrumentality and expressivity. Henley (1977, pp. 186-187) argues that "Although . . . dominance and submission gestures correspond in that they are reciprocals of similar types of behavior, one does not necessarily imply the other." My results illustrate the wisdom of Henley's contention: male displays of "dominance" in conversation do *not* necessarily generate female displays of "submission."

REFERENCES

GOFFMAN, E. 1967. Interaction Ritual: Essays on Face-to-Face Behavior. Anchor/Doubleday. Garden City, N.Y.

HENLEY, N. 1977. Body Politics: Power, Sex and Nonverbal Communication. Prentice-Hall. Englewood Cliffs, N. J.

JEFFERSON, G. 1973. A case of precision timing in ordinary conversation overlapped tag-positioned address terms in closing sequences. Semiotica **IX**:47-96.

JEFFERSON, G. & E. SCHEGLOFF. 1975. Sketch: Some orderly aspects of overlap in Natural conversation. Unpublished manuscript, Department of Sociology, University of California, Los Angeles.

KRAMER, C., B. THORNE & N. HENLEY. 1978. Perspectives on Language and Communication Signs **3**:638-651.

LAKOFF, R. 1975. Language and Women's Place. Harper & Row. New York.

MCMILLAN, J. R., A. K. CLIFTON, D. MCGRATH & W. S. GALE. 1977. Women's Language Uncertainty or Interpersonal Sensitivity and Emotionality? Sex Roles **3**:545-559.

SACKS, H., n.d. Aspects of the Sequential Organization of Conversation. Unpublished Manuscript, University of California at Irvine.

SACKS, H., E. SCHEGLOFF & G. JEFFERSON. 1974. A simplest systematics for the organization of turn-taking for conversation. Language **50**:696-735.

— The New York Times, September 7, 1977:B1.

THOMAS, W. I. 1931. The relation of research to the social process. *In* Essays on Research in the Social Sciences. The Brookings Institute. Washington, D.C.

WEST, C. 1978. Communicating Gender: A Study of Dominance and Control in Conversation. Doctoral Dissertation, Department of Sociology, University of California, Santa, Barbara.

WEST, C. & D. H. ZIMMERMAN. 1977. Women's place in everyday talk: reflections on parent-child interaction. Social Problems :521-529.

WEST, C. & D. H. ZIMMERMAN. 1978. Strangers when they meet: A study of same-sex and cross-sex conversations between unacquainted persons. Paper presented at American Sociological Association Meetings, San Francisco, California, September 4-8.

ZIMMERMAN, D. H. & C. WEST. 1975. Sex roles, interruptions and silences in conversation. *In* Language and Sex: Difference and Dominance. B. Thorne & N. Henley, Eds., Newbury House. Rowley, Mass.

APPENDIX

The transcript techniques and symbols were devised by Gail Jefferson in the course of research undertaken with Harvey Sacks. Techniques are revised, symbols added or dropped as they seem useful to the work. There is no guarantee or suggestion that the symbols of transcripts alone would permit the doing of any unspecified research tasks: they are properly used as an adjunct to the tape recorded materials.

Transcribing Conventions

Mary: I don' [know] John: [You] don't	Brackets indicate that the portions of utterances so encased are simultaneous. The left-hand bracket marks the onset of simultaneity, the right-hand bracket indicates its resolution.
A: We:::ll now	Colons indicate that the immediately prior syllable is prolonged.
A: But-	A hyphen represents a cutting off short of the immediately prior syllable.
CAPS or <u>underscoring</u>	Both of these are used to represent heavier emphasis (in speaker's pitch) on words so marked.
A: "Swat I said = B: = But you didn't	Equal signs are used to indicate that no time elapses between the objects "latched" by the marks. Often used as a transcribing convenience, it can also mean that a next speaker starts at precisely the end of a current speaker's utterance.
(1.3)	Numbers encased in parentheses indicate the seconds and tenths of seconds ensuing between speaker turns. They may also be used to indicate the duration of pauses internal to a speaker's turn.
(#)	Score sign indicates a pause of about a second that it wasn't possible to discriminate precisely.

(word)   Single parentheses with words in them indicate that something was heard, but the transcriber is not sure what it was. These can serve as a warning that the transcript may be unreliable.

((softly))   Double parentheses enclose "descriptions" not transcribed utterances.

A: I (x) I did   Parentheses encasing an "x" indicate a hitch or stutter on the part of the speaker.

A: Oh Yeah?   Punctuation marks are used for intonation, not grammar.

( )   Empty parentheses signify untimed pauses.

°So you did.   The degree symbol represents softness, or decreased amplitude.

.hh hh eh-heh   These are breathing and laughing indicators. A period followed by "hh's" marks an inhalation. The "hh's" alone stand for exhalation. The "heh's" and "henh's" are laughter syllables.

Abstract

THE ACQUISITION OF GENDERLECT

ADELAIDE HAAS

One theory of the development of gender-associated features in speech holds that children of both sexes initially learn the mother's language, but that boys shift to the use of male dialect with contact outside the home. If so, one would expect increasing differences between the sexes with age, although the age at which divergence begins or is complete has not been established. The following study by Haas investigated this issue by observing 24 children aged 4, 8, and 12 years playing in same-sex and mixed-sex dyads. Features of language, Form, Content, Topic and Use were analyzed. An advantage of Haas's design is that it provides information concerning the extent to which "genderlect" is sensitive to the sex of the conversational partner.

Of the 45 features investigated, only 8 showed sex differences that held across both age and type of dyad. Two of these features showed an increase in sex-typing with age. Three other features were typical of boys or girls at the youngest age but practically dropped out at the older ages. Five additional features varied with the sex of the play partner, but in all cases the variation occurred in the girls' speech.

The above differences occurred in only 16 of the 45 features investigated, indicating that in general the patterns of development were similar for boys and girls. No clear evidence was found for an emergence of sex-associated features with age. However, for the most part those features that emerged as sex-associated fit traditional sex stereotypes: Boys talked about sports and gave information; girls talked about sitting games and school, laughed, used few direct requests, and were compliant. Perhaps more important, however, is the variability in girls' speech as a function of the sex of the listener. Because of the small sample, this observation is only suggestive, but it indicates that the concept of "genderlect" must be broadened to include variation across contexts and conversational partners.

Editors

THE ACQUISITION OF GENDERLECT*

Adelaide Haas

*Department of Speech Communication
State University College
New Paltz, New York 12562*

Let us assume that intelligent, liberated parents of today no longer have rigid expectations for the future of their offspring. Girls are given blocks and trucks to play with and boys have their dolls—albeit frequently G.I. Joes. Girls may hope to become doctors or lawyers or engineers, rather than setting their sights on merely marrying one. Boys, as they mature, believe that they will not have the sole burden of financially supporting a family. They expect their wives to work outside the home and know that skills in cooking, cleaning, and child care are not useful to only one sex.

Progressive schools also reinforce many concepts of equality between the sexes. More men than ever are employed as teachers for the primary grades, and both shop and family living (cooking and sewing) are now courses required for both boys and girls. This was the "enlightened" contemporary environment for the present study of sex-associated features in the spoken language of elementary school children.

An hypothesis of sex differences in speech or, to use Kramer's[1] term, "genderlect" in elementary school children was proposed based on the following observations.

1. If adult men and women show variations in speech that are associated with their gender, and there is strong evidence that they do, then these variations must be acquired at some point—probably during childhood. Robin Lakoff (1975) has suggested that this acquisition occurs before age ten.

2. Middle- and upper-middle-class children as young as five-and-a-half and six years of age have demonstrated an awareness of sex role distinctions in language. Garcia-Zamor (1973) asked eight nursery school children to indicate whether a girl or boy doll uttered various sentences. Both boys and girls believed the obscenity "shit" to be male-associated, and the euphemism "drat" to be female-associated. Tag-questions such as "This is mine, isn't it?" were also female-associated. The topic of *cars* was male-associated, and negative value judgments such as "I don't like this" were female-associated. Aggressive and competitive remarks were ascribed to the

---

* This study is based on a dissertation submitted to Teachers College, Columbia University, in partial fulfillment of the Ph.D. degree. Deep appreciation is expressed to Edward Mysak, Lois Bloom, Mary Parlee, and Mark Kesselman for their useful suggestions, criticism, and encouragement. Additional thanks are given to Judith Orasanu for her helpful editorial and organizational insights.

[1] Kramer used this term in "Womens' Speech: Separate But Unequal?" Quarterly Journal of Speech. **60**:14-24, 1974. She credits Wayne Dickerson with suggesting the term.

0077-8923/0327-0101 $01.75/2 © 1979, NYAS

male doll. In general, the boy subjects were in greater agreement than the girls about whether an item was uttered by a male or female and they agreed the most when ascribing remarks to the male doll. Garcia-Zamor interpreted this greater male awareness of sex-appropriate language to mean that boys are learning a new male language, whereas girls are simply continuing to speak their mother's tongue and therefore need to be less sensitive to sex-differentiated speech.

3. Prepubertal boys and girls can typically be identified as to sex on the basis of speech alone. Sachs, Lieberman, and Erickson (1973) reported that adult judges could accurately identify the sex of children, ranging in age from four to fourteen years, from their voices. They noted that boys, in general, used lower formants, but had higher fundamental frequencies than girls. Also, boys tended to use "a more forceful definite rhythm of speaking." Since anatomical structure does not readily explain these results, the authors suggested that differences are acquired as part of the sex role in keeping with cultural expectations.

Meditch (1976) similarly found that adults can accurately judge the sex of three- to five-year-olds on the basis of tape-recorded samples of spontaneous speech. She also noted the male children were accurately categorized significantly more often than were female children, thereby concluding that boys learn sex-appropriate speech earlier than girls. This is consistent with Garcia-Zamor's interpretations of the study described earlier.

4. Further, in spite of equalitarian concepts of child rearing, parents and teachers differentially relate to boys and girls in ways which are likely to have linguistic implications. Cherry and Lewis (1977) have provided considerable evidence that caretakers of preschool children behave differentially to children of different sexes. They reported that in dyads with their two-year-old child, mothers of females talked more, used longer utterances, and repeated more child utterances than did mothers of males. Cherry (1975) noted that teachers of preschool children asked more questions of girls, but interacted more with boys and gave boys more directives.

5. Finally, some differences have already been identified in the speech of young children. Sause (1975), for example, in a study of 144 kindergarten children, found significant differences between boys and girls in 15 of 26 variables studied. Boys talked more, were more aggressive verbally, referred more to space, quantity, physical movement, self, and value judgment. Girls appeared shy, and the only category they referred to more than boys was the "female role."

Sex differences in verbosity, adjective use, and articulation and pronunciation were reported by other researchers (Bernstein, 1971; Entwisle, 1966; Maccoby, 1966; McCarthy, 1953; Winitz, 1959).

In summary, five indications of support for an hypothesis of sex differences in children are (1) men and women apparently use sex-associated styles of speech that are probably acquired before adulthood; (2) preschool children have shown an awareness of sex differentiation in language; (3) prepubertal boys and girls can be identified as to sex on the basis of speech alone; (4) caretakers differentially relate to boys and girls in ways having linguistic implications; and (5) some sex differences in children's language have already been documented.

The present study was designed to explore sex-associated spoken language in spontaneous interactions of peers. Previous studies either involved experimenter-child communications and/or were based on children's behavior in highly specific communication tasks.

A wide variety of spoken language features were analyzed for sex differences. After studing the literature and analyzing transcripts obtained during pilot study, a list of forty-five aspects of speech was compiled.

Specific features of spoken language from this list were categorized as Form, Topic, Content, or Use based on the model described by Bloom and Lahey (1978). "The *Form* of utterances can be described in terms of their acoustic, phonetic shape . . . in terms of the units of sound or phonology, the units of meaning that are words or inflections, or morphology, and the ways in which units of meaning are combined with one another, or syntax" (Bloom & Lahey, 1978, p.15). *Topic* refers to the subject matter of the spoken utterance; what the conversation is about. *Content* refers to the "categorization of the topics that are encoded in messages" such as "objects in general," "actions in general," and the "possession relation in general" (Bloom & Lahey, 1978, p.11). Content differs from Topic in that Topic refers to particular objects, events and ideas, whereas Content refers to the more general concept of how the topic is referenced. "Language *Use* consists of the socially and cognitively determined selection of behaviors according to the goals of the speaker and the context of the situation" (Bloom & Lahey, 1978, p.20). These categories of Form, Topic, Content, and Use provide a meaningful scheme for studying identifiable, yet intertwined features of speech. Definitions of features are in the APPENDIX.

In order to explore the acquisition of genderlect in many of its dimensions, the following research questions were asked:

1. Are there features of Form, Topic, Content, and Use that are sex-associated?

2. Does production of sex-associated features differ as a function of whether the speaker is in a same-sex or mixed-sex dyad?

3. Are the sexes more differentiated with increasing age by their production of sex-associated features?

METHOD

Subjects

Subjects were twenty-four normal middle- and upper-middle-class white children from the elementary school affiliated with the State University of New York at New Paltz. Four boys and four girls at age levels four-, eight-, and twelve-years were randomly selected. All children were acquainted prior to the study. Selection and pairing were done through the use of a table of random numbers.

Procedure

Two girls and two boys from an age group were brought to the laboratory at a time. This experimental group was arranged into four dyads: one all-boy dyad, one all-girl dyad, and two mixed-sex dyads. Each child participated in both a same-sex and a mixed-sex dyad.

Each dyad interacted in a playroom/waiting-room for fifteen to twenty minutes—long enough for each child to produce at least one hundred utterance units. The playroom was equipped with small tables and chairs, blackboard, chalk, eraser, paper, pencils, scissors, glue, boxes of various sizes and shapes, a ruler, a ball, and a sink. Children who were not in the playroom were engaged in various tests which they believed to be the main focus of the experiment. This procedure is a modification of one described by Garvey & BenDebba (1974).

Dyadic conversations were taped and transcribed. Two individuals were responsible for the transcription of each of the twenty-four tapes. They had to agree completely on what was uttered before it could be included in the transcription. Both video and audio tapes were used. The video recording enabled transcribers to identify the speakers; audio tape was more intelligible. All transcripts were later checked by a third person for accuracy. One-hundred percent agreement was required. The time in minutes for each subject to produce one hundred utterance units in each dyad was recorded, and each utterance unit was numbered one to one hundred for each speaker in each dyad. An utterance unit is "a stretch of one person's speech bounded by the partner's speech or by a pause of 1.0 second or more" (Garvey & BenDebba, 1974, p.1160). Through pilot study, it was decided that one hundred utterance units by each subject in each dyad were sufficient to obtain a sample of sex-associated features. This would also provide a comparable corpus for each subject in each situation.

All identifying information such as speaker's name and sex was removed from all transcripts. These cleaned transcripts were then given to another individual for analysis.

Analysis

The analysis required classifying each utterance unit four times, for Form, Topic, Content, and Use. Within each of these categories it was determined which feature of spoken language, from the previously prepared list, was produced. (See APPENDIX for detail of the categorization scheme.)

In order to determine the reliability of this method of analysis all utterances from a mixed-sex dyad were independently analyzed by the researcher, four student assistants, and a male professor of English unfamiliar with the purpose of this study. All participated in a training session first, and were given a list of relevant definitions. Overall estimated reliability as determined by the Sander's Agreement Index (Agreement Index = Number of agreements/Agreements + Disagreements) was 90 percent.

RESULTS

Overall Sex Differences

The first question was directed at the investigation of overall sex differences. "Are there features of Form, Topic, Content, and Use which are sex-associated?" All the boys' scores could not be directly compared to all the girls' scores because subjects on each day interacted in the dyads making each subject's scores dependent on the scores of the other subjects of that day. Therefore, the scores for each feature of both boys on each experimental day were summed and compared to the sum of the girls' scores for each feature on that day. A t-test for dependent pairs was used to compare the six matched sets of boys and girls. Levels of significance reported in the text are at the .05 probability level or better.

TABLE 1 (see APPENDIX) shows means and standard deviations of spoken language features by sex, dyad, and age. Only those features for which differences were apparent are included. The superscript § by a feature marks overall sex differences.

Form

When age and dyad were not considered, no significant sex differences in frequency of utterance of any features of Form were identified.

Topic

Sports was referenced significantly more by males for all ages and dyads taken together. School and the "experimental situation" were referenced significantly more by females.

Content

Perceptual attributes, functional attributes, and location were features produced significantly more often by boys. Girls did not utter any features of content significantly more than males across age and dyad.

Use

Main effects of sex were found for information-giving (male-associated) and compliance (female-associated).

Dyadic Influences on Sex Differences

The second question asked, "Does production of sex-associated features differ as a function of whether the speaker is in a same-sex or mixed-sex dyad?" The scores for each spoken language feature by two boys in a same-sex dyadic interaction were pooled and compared with scores obtained by two girls of the same age level in a same-sex dyadic interaction. A t-test for independent groups was used to compare the six boy dyads with the six girl dyads. Each boy subject also had been randomly paired with a same-aged girl. Since the utterances of each child might be influenced by the speech of the partner, each mixed-sex dyad was treated as a dependent pair. Boys' scores in the mixed-sex dyads were compared with girls' scores in the mixed-sex dyads. T-tests were used to determine the statistical significance of the differences.

Features with superscript ¶ in TABLE 1 showed significant sex differences in same-sex or mixed-sex dyads.

Form

Sex-associated differences in Form occurred only in mixed-sex dyads. Girls laughed significantly more than boys only when paired with a boy. No significant differences were found in Form when comparing all-boy and all-girl dyads.

Topic

Sex-differences in Topic were found in both same-sex and mixed-sex dyads. In both conditions, boys talked significantly more about sports, although for boys this Topic was referenced more often when two boys were paired together.

Girls in same-sex dyads talked significantly more about school than boys in same-sex dyads. Not statistically significant but noteworthy were the girls' high frequency of reference to sitting games in same-sex dyads at the older age levels.

Content

Significant sex-differences in referring to identity, location, and wishing/needing were found only in same-sex dyads. Boys referenced location more; girls spoke more about identity and wishing and needing. No significant differences in Content were found when boys and girls were paired. However, negative value judgments were made most often by young girls in mixed-sex dyads.

Use

As with Form, significant sex-differences in Use of spoken language occurred only in mixed-sex dyads. Direct requests were sex-associated for boys, and compliance was sex-associated for girls.

Development of Sex Differences

Question three asked, "Are the sexes more differentiated with increasing age by their production of sex-associated features?" Although these differences could not be treated statistically because of small sample sizes, TABLE 1 summarizes the means for each age group. The superscript # in TABLE 1 next to a feature denotes an apparent age by sex effect. In general the pattern for one sex paralleled the pattern for the other sex.

Form

Both boys and girls tended to laugh (female-associated) more and use sound effects (male-associated) less with increased age. The most laughter was produced by eight-and twelve-year-old girls in mixed-sex dyads.

Twelve-year-old boys laughed as much as girls, but only in same-sex dyads. Sound effects were produced primarily by four-year-old boys regardless of dyad.

Topic

Sitting games were spoken about most by twelve-year old girls when paired with another girl. Sports, which was male-associated, was talked about most by both sexes at the eight-year-old level. At twelve years boys continued to talk about sports but only with other boys. Four-year-old boys in both dyadic conditions spoke more about motors than older boys or girls of any age did. No age pattern for references to school or the experimental situation was observed in same-sex dyads, although in mixed-sex dyads both topics were spoken about most in the twelve-year-old group by both boys and girls.

Content

No clear age patterns were found for either sex in reference to identity or location.

Functional attributes were referenced most by boys in the same-sex dyads at ages eight and twelve. Girls in mixed-sex dyads had a similar pattern, although to a lesser extent. Girls made the most negative value judgments at age four in mixed-sex dyads; at the older age levels the frequency of these utterances was similar to that for boys in both experimental conditions. Girls spoke of wishing/needing more than boys at age four; the difference between the sexes decreased with age.

Use

Both sexes tended to make the most direct requests (male-associated) at the youngest age level in both dyad conditions; girls in mixed-sex dyads made the fewest direct requests at all ages.

Eight-year old boys gave the most information (male-associated) to male peers. For girls information giving decreased with age in same-sex dyads.

Girls in both dyad conditions and boys in mixed-sex dyads were most verbally compliant (female-associated) at age twelve. The female pattern in same-sex dyads most clearly showed increased compliance with age

DISCUSSION

Meditch (1975) notes that by "age three both boys and girls have developed their respective patterns well enough to be identified solely on the basis of speech" (p.421). She postulates that boys learn sex-specific patterns earlier than girls, and that boys' development of male-associated spoken language consists of *losing* features they exhibited earlier, whereas girls must first lose certain features, then acquire female-marked patterns.

Lakoff (1975) believes that both boys and girls first learn "women's language" and use this until about age five. By around ten years of age, "boys have unlearned their original form of expression and adopted new forms of expression, while the girls retain their old ways of speech" (p.6).

Do boys unlearn certain features between ages five and ten, while they learn new ones as Lakoff suggests? In the present study, boys used fewer sound effects at the older age levels. This however does not reflect unlearning women's language but rather a change in activity, since sound effects were an accompaniment to early imaginative play. There was no evidence that female features diminished with age for the boys studied, or that male features increased with age. In fact, in the present study, girls seemed to lose a male-associated feature with age (information giving to same-sex peers). Girls showed a tendency with age to increase their production of the following female-associated features: Form: laughter, Topics: sitting games, school, and the experimental situation, and Use: compliance. As they got older, girls expressed less negative evaluation and wishing/needing. With the above exceptions, features that increased in frequency with age for one sex paralleled the pattern for the other sex.

Conclusions

Some evidence was found in the present study for an increase in gender-associated speech in girls between the ages of four and twelve. Boys by age four already seemed to use male-associated spoken language.

Age trends were observed for both sexes in each of the categories Form, Topic, Content, and Use. Since the trends were generally roughly parallel for boys and girls, it is likely that language development between ages four and twelve follows a similar pattern for both girls and boys. Exceptions to this are the downward trend by girls in same-sex dyads to give information and an increase in the use of compliant remarks by girls in both same-sex and mixed-sex dyads, with a weaker pattern for boys.

The influence of the gender of the communication partner is significant, and needs to be studied further. Form and Use differences occurred primarily in mixed-sex dyads. This suggests the importance of sex-role in mixed-sex interactions. Males may relate to males in much the same way that females relate to females, however roles become defined when individuals are with members of the opposite sex. These roles are reflected in language Use with males playing the dominant part by giving information and making direct requests and the females being subordinate as seen in their greater use of compliant utterances. The Form of laughter may also be seen within this framework, since there were no significant differences in laughter in same-sex dyads, but girls laughed more when with boys. In a sense, this is compliance or support of male-initiated humor.

Content and Topic differences tended to be more pronounced in same-sex dyads. This suggests a greater sharing of interests among same-sex peers.

More information is needed however, especially for the early years, in order to elucidate a chronology of acquisition of sex-associated spoken language.

REFERENCES

BERNSTEIN, B. Language and roles. 1971. *In* Language Acquisition: Models and Methods. R. Huxley & Ingram, Eds. Academic Press. New York.

BLOOM, L. & M. LAHEY. 1978. Language Development and Language Disorders. John Wiley & Sons. New York.

CHERRY, L. J. 1975. Teacher-child verbal interaction: An approach to the study of sex differences. *In* Language and Sex: Difference and Dominance. B. Thorne & N. Henley, Eds. Newbury House. Rowley, Mass.

CHERRY, L.J. & M. LEWIS. 1977. Differential socialization of girls and boys: Implications for sex differences in language development. *In* Development of Communication: Social and Pragmatic Factors in Language Acquisition. C. Snow & N. Waterson, Eds. John Wiley & Sons. New York.

ENTWISLE, D. R. 1966. The word associations of young children. John Hopkins Press. Baltimore, Md.

GARCIA-ZAMOR, M. A. 1973. Child awareness of sex-role distinctions in language use. Paper presented at the Linguistic Society of America Meeting, December 1973.

GARVEY, C. & M. BENDEBBA. 1974. Effects of age, sex and partner on children's dyadic speech. Child Development **45:**1159-1161.

LAKOFF, R. 1975. Language and Woman's Place. Harper Colophon. New York.

MACCOBY, E. E., Ed. 1966. The Development of Sex Differences. Stanford University Press. Stanford, Ca.

McCARTHY, D. 1953. Some possible explanations of sex differences in language development and disorders. Journal of Psychology **35:**155-160.

MEDITCH, A. 1975. The development of sex-specific speech patterns in young children. Anthropological Linguistics **17:**421-433.

SACHS, J., P. LIEBERMAN & D. ERICKSON. 1973. Anatomical and cultural determinants of male and female speech. *In* Language Attitudes: Current Trends and Prospects. R. W. Shuy & R. W. Fasold, Eds. Georgetown University Press. Washington, D.C.

SAUSE, E. F. 1976. Computer content analysis of sex differences in the language of children. Journal of Psycholinguistic Research **5:**311-324.

SLOBIN, D. 1967. A Field Manual for Cross-Cultural Study of the Acquisition of Communicative Competence. University of California Press. Berkeley.

WINITZ, H. 1959. Language skills of male and female kindergarten children. Journal of Speech and Hearing Research **2:**377-391.

APPENDIX

DEFINITION OF TERMS

FORM

Laughter: An audible nonverbal response to humor. Giggle.
Crying: An audible nonverbal expression of sadness or pain. Weeping. Sobbing.
Screams: Sharp, piercing, nonverbal utterances. Yells.
Involuntary vocalizations: Any of several nonverbal sounds such as coughing or throat clearing.

Sound effects: Vocalizations used in association with objects, movements, etc. Includes onomatopoeia, e.g.: "Brrm" goes the car.

Singing, whistling: Words or sounds uttered musically.

Phatic, perfunctory: Words or expressions used ritualistically—not to be interpreted literally, e.g.: "Hi." "How are you?"

Politeness: Words or phrases used to express courteousness, e.g.: "Please," "Thank you," "You're welcome."

Name calling: Derogatory epithets, e.g.: "You dummy."

Slang: Words or phrases in current usage, not part of traditional speech, e.g.: "Far out," "Tough," "Yup." Does not include "Yeah," "Okay."

Expressiveness: Exclamations such as "Oh," "Wow," "Gee."

Profanity/obscenity: Swear words, blasphemous or irreverant expressions . . . indecent or lewd language.

Soft profanity: Euphemistic expressions for profanity or obscenity, such as "Gosh," "Shucks," "Heck."

Unfinished sentences: Sentences left dangling by the speaker—does not include those unfinished as the result of an interruption or mazes clarified by the speaker within the same utterance.

Sentences: Complete statements which would be marked by a period in written form. Includes declaratives and imperatives.

Questions: Inquiries, interrogatives that would be marked by a question mark in written form.

Other forms: Anything unclassifiable above. May not contain a subject and a predicate. Includes one-word utterances, e.g.: "Yes," "No," "Okay," "There."

TOPIC

Sitting games: Reference to or conversation concerning structured games with rules, which do not require full body movement, e.g.: cards, chess, monopoly.

Arts & crafts: Reference to or conversation concerning aesthetic work. Includes drawing, coloring, painting, sculpture in clay, paper, wood, etc.

Sports: References to or conversation concerning outdoor or athletic activities.

Motors/vehicles/weapons: Reference to or conversation concerning machines, mechanical devices, gadgets, cars, trucks, planes, guns, sling-shots, etc.

Home: Reference to a place or residence.

School: Reference to the educational establishment such as building, classes, teachers, homework.

Money: Reference to price, cost, dollars, cents, etc.

Clothes/attire: Reference to dress and objects worn.

People: Reference to friends, classmates, family members, etc. People other than self.

Holidays/vacations: Reference to festivities, commemorative days, days off from school, etc.

Experimental situation: Reference to activities related to participation in this experiment.

Other: Reference to topics not included above.

CONTENT

Action: Focus is on expressing movement or activity.

Identity of objects or persons: Focus is on labeling—name only. Who.

Perceptual attributes: Focus is on describing visual, audible, and other perceptual qualities of an object, person or place—includes age.

Functional attributes: Focus is on describing uses of an object, person, or place. Includes scores in games.

Location: Focus is on where something is or occurred. "Here." "There." Use this category over action, when place is the emphasis.

Positive value judgments: Focus is on approving of a person, place, object, or event. Includes feelings, "Do you like...?"

Negative value judgments: Focus is on disapproving of a person, place, object, or event. "Do you hate...?" "He's dumb."

Wishing/needing: Focus is on expressing a desire for a person, place, object, or event.

Pretending: Focus is on making believe or engaging in imaginative play.

Other: Focus not classifiable above...wonder, thinking, owning, etc.

USE

Information giving: Intent of utterance is to impart knowledge or information. Teaching, lecturing, e.g.: "This is a book."

Information seeking: Intent of utterance is to request information, e.g.: "What is that?"

Direct request for action: Intent is to get the other person to do something, e.g.: "Give me the book."

Indirect request: Intent is to get the other person to do something but the statement needs interpreting, e.g.: "You walk too fast." (Means: slow down). Also asking permission, "Let me have a turn," "You want to clear the table."

Tentative: Suggests uncertainty, hedging, conditionality. Forms include tag questions, "It's hot, isn't it?"; hypotheses, "I think it's hot"; qualifiers, "It's sort of hot."

Compliant/agreeing/supportive: Intent is to go along with or support the other person, e.g.: "Yeah," "Sure," "Okay," "That's a good idea."

Assertion/disagreeing: Intent is to oppose the other person, e.g.; "I'm going to hit you."

Inadequacy: Intent is to convey lack of knowledge or inability, e.g.: "I don't know," "I can't," "I'll fail."

Other: Uses not classifiable above.

TABLE 1

MEANS AND STANDARD DEVIATIONS OF SPOKEN LANGUAGE FEATURES
BY SEX, DYAD, AND AGE

Category Feature	Sex	Dyad	Age Groups*		
			Four-Years	Eight-Years	Twelve-Ye
Form					
Laugh¶,#	M	SS†	5.50 (4.44)	3.50 (3.11)	10.00 (4.€
		MS‡	1.25 (1.89)	2.50 (5.00)	5.50 (3.5
	F	SS	1.00 (0.82)	3.50 (2.89)	9.50 (11.0
		MS	5.75 (4.11)	11.50 (1.92)	10.75 (8.0
Sound effects#	M	SS	5.25 (5.06)	1.50 (1.00)	0.00 (0.0
		MS	4.50 (2.52)	2.50 (0.58)	0.00 (0.0
	F	SS	0.00 (0.00)	1.00 (0.82)	0.00 (0.0
		MS	1.25 (1.50)	0.00 (0.00)	0.25 (0.5
Topic					
Sitting games¶,#	M	SS	0.00 (0.00)	0.25 (0.50)	1.50 (1.9
		MS	0.75 (1.50)	0.00 (0.00)	0.25 (0.5
	F	SS	0.50 (1.00)	5.75 (6.95)	30.00 (21.€
		MS	1.25 (2.50)	2.25 (4.50)	2.00 (2.4
Sports§,¶,#	M	SS	1.25 (1.50)	74.75 (7.14)	51.50 (7.4
		MS	1.25 (2.50)	37.50 (19.60)	9.75 (11.2
	F	SS	0.00 (0.00)	8.25 (12.82)	4.25 (4.€
		MS	0.00 (0.00)	23.00 (11.78)	7.25 (8.0
Motors#	M	SS	19.25 (23.06)	0.00 (0.00)	0.00 (0.0
		MS	11.00 (12.70)	2.25 (2.87)	0.00 (0.0
	F	SS	0.50 (0.58)	3.00 (1.41)	0.00 (0.0
		MS	1.25 (2.50)	1.25 (1.50)	0.00 (0.0
School§,¶	M	SS	1.25 (1.50)	1.25 (1.89)	0.00 (0.€
		MS	0.50 (1.00)	1.00 (2.00)	12.25 (21.
	F	SS	5.25 (5.56)	6.00 (8.49)	6.75 (2.2
		MS	4.00 (6.73)	3.75 (3.68)	16.50 (22.7
Experimental situation§,#	M	SS	6.50 (0.58)	3.75 (2.50)	5.50 (5.4
		MS	0.50 (1.00)	5.50 (5.20)	25.00 (15.
	F	SS	10.00 (6.83)	8.00 (0.82)	16.00 (9.7
		MS	1.00 (1.41)	7.75 (5.06)	24.50 (11.€
Content					
Identity¶	M	SS	9.50 (3.00)	6.25 (4.19)	8.75 (4.
		MS	12.25 (2.87)	12.75 (2.99)	10.50 (2.€

Note: Maximum possible frequency for any feature = 100.
*Total number of subjects (N) = 24; four boys and four girls in each age group.

~gory~ ~re~	Sex	Dyad	Age Groups*		
			Four-Years	Eight-Years	Twelve-Years
	F	SS	11.25 (6.34)	11.00 (4.08)	16.25 (5.74)
		MS	8.25 (4.65)	13.75 (0.96)	7.00 (5.35)
~ptual~ ~utes~§,#	M	SS	7.00 (3.56)	6.25 (2.87)	12.00 (2.94)
		MS	12.25 (6.13)	7.00 (3.92)	9.50 (5.75)
	F	SS	3.00 (2.45)	7.25 (2.99)	3.75 (4.99)
		MS	5.25 (2.50)	5.50 (3.70)	9.50 (3.11)
~tional~ ~utes~§,#	M	SS	2.00 (0.82)	13.75 (5.85)	10.50 (4.93)
		MS	4.50 (5.45)	4.75 (3.10)	4.50 (6.46)
	F	SS	1.25 (1.50)	5.00 (2.16)	2.00 (2.71)
		MS	1.75 (2.36)	6.50 (3.87)	5.75 (5.12)
~tion~§,¶	M	SS	8.75 (3.86)	9.00 (6.38)	6.25 (3.20)
		MS	3.25 (6.50)	4.00 (1.16)	4.00 (2.16)
	F	SS	5.25 (3.30)	5.75 (2.22)	1.50 (1.29)
		MS	3.00 (2.16)	4.00 (1.83)	3.75 (2.99)
~tive~ ~ation~¶,#	M	SS	7.25 (4.57)	7.00 (2.58)	9.00 (4.55)
		MS	8.25 (8.46)	12.75 (4.57)	8.00 (6.33)
	F	SS	9.25 (5.50)	6.75 (3.78)	9.25 (4.65)
		MS	16.75 (18.04)	14.25 (5.25)	8.50 (5.20)
~ing/~ ~ng~	M	SS	2.75 (3.59)	0.75 (1.50)	0.75 (0.96)
		MS	1.50 (1.00)	2.50 (2.52)	1.25 (1.26)
	F	SS	6.50 (2.08)	4.25 (2.06)	2.00 (1.63)
		MS	6.75 (9.61)	0.50 (0.58)	1.50 (1.00)
~t~ ~st~¶,#	M	SS	11.50 (7.55)	8.50 (8.43)	7.50 (3.79)
		MS	10.25 (4.99)	10.25 (4.99)	6.00 (8.72)
	F	SS	11.25 (5.74)	8.50 (6.25)	9.75 (6.50)
		MS	7.25 (4.35)	4.00 (2.94)	4.50 (3.70)
~nation~ ~§,#~	M	SS	33.75 (11.96)	45.25 (17.21)	29.75 (12.29)
		MS	34.00 (13.52)	38.75 (9.88)	37.50 (12.69)
	F	SS	35.50 (8.06)	32.75 (11.59)	22.50 (9.85)
		MS	33.25 (10.53)	28.00 (11.86)	31.00 (18.13)
~liance/~ ~rtive~	M	SS	8.75 (2.99)	12.50 (13.18)	7.00 (4.32)
		MS	6.25 (3.78)	8.00 (5.83)	10.00 (5.89)
	F	SS	6.75 (6.02)	11.50 (4.80)	17.50 (2.89)
		MS	11.00 (8.89)	10.75 (4.03)	16.50 (6.03)

~e-sex.~   ‡ Mixed-sex.   § Main effect of sex.   ¶ Effect of dyad.   # Effect of age.

113

LANGUAGE, SEX AND GENDER: DOES *LA DIFFÉRENCE* MAKE A DIFFERENCE? DISCUSSION

Jessie Bernard

Research Scholar, Honoris Causa
Pennsylvania State University
University Park, Pennsylvania 16802

The sub-title of this workshop asks whether "la différence" makes a difference. If the context of the question did not make quite clear what difference was intended, one might well ask, *what* difference? Greater male tendency toward baldness? Hemophilia? Color blindness? Greater female viability? Clearly none of these is meant. One of the questions asked of participants specified the difference intended, namely: "are men and women differentiated by the content, structure, or use of speech?" The answer came through clear and loud in all the papers: yes, they are, there are differences between the sexes in the use of speech. They are not, however, based on primitive biological sex but on sex-role socialization. How? the second question addressed to participants asked. How are gender differences in language behavior socialized? Two papers (Beatty, Haas) addressed this question. Differences based on socialization imply that change is possible. There was, however, relatively little attention paid to the third question posed by the workshop: what is the relation between language change and social change? two papers (Lakoff, Gregersen) spoke to this question, both casually. One (Gregersen) did not see language change as a useful feminist technique for producing social change and the other (Lakoff) capitulated to the male style.

Before I proceed to discuss the papers, I must make it clear that I approach the subjects here discussed as a consumer rather than as a producer of research in this area. I am not credentialed to make a serious technical critique of any of the papers. "Syntactics," "semantics," and "pragmatics," except in the non-technical, everyday meanings of the terms, are *terra incognita* to me.

Lakoff underscores the old cliché that style is the man and, presumably, the woman. She believes a person's style applies across the psychic range, characterizing cognition, perception, interpersonal strategies, and physical activity. And she attempts to apply the conceptualization of rules of linguistic behavior to style so conceptualized. She is looking, in brief, for the "grammar" of style. She selects a parameter which she calls "mode of rapport" and distinguishes four styles. She hypothesizes that two of them—clarity and distance—are associated with males and two—deference and camaraderie—with females. She does not see these styles or modes of rapport as categorical but as points on a gradient so that one may have

115

0077-8923/79/0327-0115 $01.75/2 ©1979, NYAS

styles that fall between the several categories. Her task is "to make predictions, to show that there are rules governing these stylistic entities, so that it is natural, expectable, and predictable, given certain theoretical assumptions, that these traits [of women's style] occur together, and not others."

I find the "rules" governing mode of rapport interesting and I can recognize each style. I know people who follow the clarity style; they seem to be talking to themselves. They are invulnerable to clues of boredom in their listeners. They seem to be wound up and incapable of stopping until they have said it all, made it perfectly clear. They have never heard the old adage that we learn because we love the teacher. If the chairperson tries to stop them, they sail on undaunted, unaware that they are stealing other people's time. I would not, though, categorize Rhett Butler as using the clarity style. His "frankly, my dear, I don't give a damn" tells us—contrary to the clarity rule—a lot about his state of mind and his attitude toward Scarlett.

I know people who follow the distance rules also. The distance may be vertical as well as spatial, figuratively speaking. They talk down. Or up. They vary the distance.

So far so good. I have a little more difficulty with the rules of deference. Huxley thought Darwin was too deferential toward his critics. C.H. Cooley, on the other hand, believed that it was precisely Darwin's deference to his readers that made for clarity and hence persuasiveness:

> . . .Probably few thoughtful and open-minded persons can read the *Origin of Species* without becoming Darwinists, yielding willingly, for the time at least, to his ascendancy, and feeling him as a master. If we consider the traits that give him this authority, it will be found that . . . as we read his chapters, and begin to build him up in our imaginations out of the subtle suggestions of style, we find ourselves thinking of him as, first of all, a true and simple man, a patient, sagacious seeker after the real. This makes us . . . feel at home with him, forget suspicion, and incline to believe as he believes, even if we fail to understand his reasons . . ." (pp. 337-338).

Cooley thought that Darwin was involved with his readers, did try to establish rapport. Teddy Roosevelt is said to have answered the question of how he maintained such good rapport with his public by saying that he wrote to an audience of men sitting around the stove in a country store. He involved them. It is thus hard for me to characterize the rules of deference as stereotypically female. There is, of course, also the use of deference by males as a form of dominance, as when the knight put his lady on a pedestal and deferred her completely out of the picture, and the whole courtesy and chivalric tradition that until recently led men to show deference toward women, thus reducing rather than building rapport. There is, further, the conceptualization of deference as, in effect, tribute, as in Randall Collins' market-model of conversation:

> . . . everyone gravitates toward those things in which he can get the best deference deal. This depends on his opportunities, resources, native capacities, and competition from others . . . . Everyone moves toward the

> best available exchanges for creating his subjective status. But by no means
> is everyone able to get others to help him create a conversational world in
> which he can continuously show off, receive deference, and enjoy himself.
> Some persons must settle for lesser realities in which they are merely au-
> diences and supporters of conversational heroes . . . . Where one stands
> depends on the resources that he brings to the market . . . .(pp.135, 136).

Or deference, in the market model, may be a "resource of weakness," the
price one pays for the privilege of even being admitted to the conversation
(p.136).

The rules of camaraderie are easy for me to understand. But in the present state of flux I sometimes find myself puzzled. In letters, how to salute
the person I am writing to; how to sign off? I have a hard time remembering
names; when I am introduced to a group of people it is much easier to
remember only one. First names are usually easier. So first names it is right
off, even with strangers. The "diffusion" of this style from West to East is
interesting. In fact, cultivating camaraderie has become, almost, a growth
industry in California.

I am most uncertain about the association of clarity and distance with
men and deference and camaraderie with women. It seems analogous to the
instrumental-male and expressive-female contrast propounded by Parsons
and Bales (1955). There is, to be sure, evidence from psychology that there
are differences in sociality between men and women, men showing more
separatism, women more communion (Bardwick, 1974). Despite this
separatism, we have the phenomenon of male bonding as well, despite
Tiger's doubts, of female bonding. I am also a little surprised to see detail-
orientation as male and "the big picture" as female. Isn't the usual
stereotype just the reverse? the female being detail-oriented and the male
showing the wide perspective?

Lakoff's cross-cultural examples make her point but they do not tally
with, let us say, Kurt Lewin's comparison between Germans and Americans
(sex unspecified). He noted that Germans were more distant in early contacts and Americans far more camaraderie-oriented. But once the German
let down his defense he was capable of far greater intimacy than American
men who rarely get to a level of true intimacy. The cultural variable is an interesting one. In a book I once called among the most influential of its
time—early 1930s—found on the shelves of almost all college students,
Ruth Benedict delineated for us three "patterns of culture." The concept
"pattern" was analogous to Lakoff's "styles." These patterns or styles or
rules pervaded all aspects of the culture; they formed a "coherent picture."
The theory of diffusion popular in those days also stated that a culture trait
had to fit into a culture's pattern if it was to be accepted, thus serving in a
way a predictive function. Cultures selected traits they could use and
discarded others (p.41). Such patterns were coherent, carrying the same
motif in all modalities (pp. 43-44). ". . . cultural behavior
. . . tends . . . to be integrated. A culture, like an individual, is a more or

less consistent pattern of thought and action . . . ."(p. 42). Her discussion of "patterns" might well have been called a "grammar of culture." I note parenthetically that the mental-pathology model seems quite tempting in connection with cultural phenomena. Lakoff finds the Shapiro (reference) concept of neurotic styles in terms of mode of attentiveness a useful model and violations of personal styles schizophrenic. Benedict also characterized cultures as paranoid and schizophrenic. I might add that sometimes departing from personal style may be viewed as humorous rather than pathological. On the stage, for example, it is always funny when, let us say, a ballerina steps out of character or style and begins to tap dance. Or the rock singer turns suddenly operatic.

Also in the culture tradition was Margaret Mead's *Sex and Temperament in Three Primitive Societies,* perhaps the most wanted book of the century. She found both male and female Arapesh to be "feminine"; all Mundugumor to be "masculine"; and the Tchambouli, to show reversal of Western gender stereotypes. My critique of this book was, for all intents and purposes, ignored. I found that her own data did not support her conclusions. The relevance of these comments here is to show that sex-differences in style or rules of rapport have been conceptualized as pertaining to both sexes of whole cultures and deserve at least a bow in Lakoff's discussion.

A number of interesting points must be ignored here but one is of such major importance that it cannot be passed over. It has, in effect, to do with the sociology of knowledge. Lakoff tells us that women's style has been viewed as deviant as compared to the normal human style; it has not been granted autonomy in its own right, as men's has. Women have, in DeBeauvoir's words, been the Other. In recent years, women in all the social-science disciplines have been pointing out how deficient their areas of learning are because of their male bias. Knowledge, they point out, has been a male prerogative. It deals with subjects of interest to men, is seen through a male prism, either leaves women out or deals with them only as they fit into the male world. I recently attended a conference on *The Prism of Sex: Equity in the Pursuit of Knowledge.* Ten women in seven disciplines ranging from theology through history, political science, philosophy, psychology, sociology, and literature, documented in detail the lacunae and distortions resulting from the absence of research on women. Catharine Stimpson, editor of *Signs,* spoke of the Power to Name, a linguistic power that men have had but not women.

Gregersen's paper on male insults in over a hundred languages illustrates the male bias in his discipline. Not until well along in his paper did we learn that he was talking only about male insults and that none of his informants were women so that a whole area of insults was omitted. Not that his results are any the less interesting and important for that. It was the cavalier assumption that omitting the world of female insult was not important; the only data that counted were about males. The data themselves were fascinating, especially the apparently disproportionate part played by mothers in the insult repertoire of the men. I am always amazed when, by way of research, I catch a glimpse of the male sexual mentality. Elsie Clews Parsons noted a long time ago that the sex vocabulary of women was inadequate for discussing even her own sexuality, let alone male sexuality. The richness not only of vocabulary but also of figures of speech in the male sex mentality is striking to me, and, presumably to a great many other women as well. Insult by way of fathers were reported less common. Either because the father's body must have been less strange, or less identified with the recipient of the insulted, or less mysterious, or more familiar or because of some other reason, it did not have the power to hurt that insults involving the mother's body did. It occurs to me, whether it has any significance or not, that in this country fathers become involved when admirable traits are being dealt with rather than insults. Thus my father is bigger, smarter, richer, a better baseball player, or what-have-you than yours. It is the "dirty dozens" that involve the mother.

On the more theoretical side, Gregersen dealt, if only tangentially, with the question of the relation between language and social change. He tended to believe that it was social change that brought about language change rather than vice versa. True, we had now changed Negro to Black and homosexual to gay, but there has been little actual corresponding social change. Nor were sex pronouns important, as witnessed by the experience of Turkey and USSR. He was, therefore, not convinced that the feminist attack on the use of the male pronoun was destined to change anything. True, one may say in reply, it might not get the ERA ratified in any of the three remaining states. But it has surely raised the consciousness of a lot of people.

The paper by John Beatty tackles the basic question of the interplay between biology and roles. He presents three alternatives for defining sex-related roles: (1) they are behaviors identified or caused by biological sex; (2) they are behaviors identified with a social status; or (3) behavior that occurs during the sex act. Beatty solves the conceptualizing problem by distinguishing role (masculinity, femininity) from sexuality. The masculinity-femininity category we have no difficulty with. Beatty sees them as the image we have for males and females. But conceptualization of our sexuality has a peculiar "obligatory gap" in it. For although there is a word for male sexuality—virility—there is, Beatty tells us, no cognate word for female sexuality. "The very concept which it would identify would be exactly that which would inhibit women from being feminine." I am intrigued at this "almost obligatory gap" in our language today. I think there were such terms in Chaucer's time. I propose, now that female sexuality has been resuscitated, that we use "orgasmicity" to fill the gap.

The ambiguity with respect to the terms "lady" and "woman" is interesting also. In a footnote in a book published in 1971, I said: "There is . . . [little] consensus with respect to the term *Lady*. In Victorian times a lady was a special kind of person, refined, circumspect, noble, virtuous, sexless, well behaved, and well mannered. Both the term and the concept went out of fashion in the twentieth century. Modern women did not want to be ladies; to be called 'ladylike' came to be something to be resented. It has been with some surprise, therefore, that I have noted a return to the use of this term even by fellow social scientists in research conferences. They speak of research subjects as 'ladies,' as though at a loss for what else to call women (p. 7)." The trend among feminists is to reject the use of lady as implying weakness. Beatty is quite correct in the implications of sexlessness in the concept of lady; but woman does not necessarily imply sexuality. It might imply strength. Or, as in Wordsworth's poem, "a perfect woman, nobly planned, to warn, to comfort, and command." Note: "command."

I might add that I have myself become increasingly distressed by the term "role" as it has come to be used in both social psychology and sociology. In a book published in 1957, I built the discussion of social problems on the basis of role and status as conceptualized by Ralph Linton and by Robert Bales. I used both group-role and institutional-role as the units. Both conceive of roles as functional. Since that time the concept, especially as applied to the sexes, has burgeoned out of all proportion. It has come to mean all things to all men—and women. Every author has to tell us how he/she is using it. I have about arrived at the conclusion that we would do well to junk it entirely.

The last two papers are primarily reports of specific research projects. West's deals with adults, the other one deals with children.

I think West's use of conversational interruptions as analogous to rape is a stroke of genius. Her laboratory observations show that although men interrupt women more than women interrupt men, the women do not "ask for it" or take it lying down, no pun intended. I think she is on to something here. But I am sure she would be the first to note that her findings call for further extension. Her subjects this time were college students, already a biased sample, almost an avant garde. This study, like Lakoff's must be seen in comparative perspective. For example, I mentioned the West study to a friend of mine who was reared in a Jewish immigrant home. She told me how incredible it was when, at school, she was taught not to discuss religion or politics in social gatherings. Such vivacious discussions were what life was all about. She reveled in them, among both men and women. She expected to interrupt and to be interrupted. If you waited for your turn you might never get a chance. It was a free-for-all and the best man—or woman—got the floor. Interruptions in such a setting under the rules of that game meant you were part of the game. If you did not interrupt, did not fight for the floor, withdrew from the fray, then you were out of it, not, in fact, a member of the group. It might even be a sign of disapproval, hostility, annoyance. The kinds of interruption West has studied belong to the take-turns model. Not all people subscribe to it.

I am always personally appreciative whenever a researcher reviews the literature on a subject with which my own acquaintance is quite peripheral. Haas' summary of the work on genderlect in children is, therefore, useful to me and, presumably, to others.

Haas rightly warns us that we must be wary of category labels and look beyond stereotypes and that quick categorization may lead to false stereotyping. Yet, it seems to me that she herself has fallen into this fallacy in her own analyses and interpretations. I would—simply to clarify my point—like to re-interpret her own data. Haas finds that information-giving becomes increasingly a feature found in boys and compliance a feature found in girls. Haas sees these as reflecting differences in dominance and compliance. However, where Haas sees a difference in dominance and compliance one might just as legitimately see less and greater maturity. The greater deference and concern for the companion which Haas sees as compliance may, again, be an index of greater maturity. And so on for other differences interpreted in what I consider stereotyped patterns. With respect to her data there can be no serious objection; it is in her interpretation of them that the questions can be raised.

REFERENCES

BALES, R. F. 1955. Role differentiation in small decision making groups. See Parsons and Bales.

BARDWICK, J. 1974. Androgyny and humanistic goals. *In* The American Woman: Who Will, She He? M. L. McBee & K. H. Blake Eds. Glencoe Press. Beverly Hills.

BENEDICT, R. 1934. Patterns of Culture. Penguin. New York.

BERNARD, J. 1945. Observation and generalization in cultural anthropology. American Journal of Sociology 50:284-291.

— 1957. Social Problems at Midcentury. Dryden Press. New York.

— 1971. Women and the Public Interest. Aldine. Chicago.

BLOCK, J. H. 1975. Another look at sex differentiation in the socialization behaviors of mothers and fathers. Draft of paper for conference on New Directions for Research on Women, Madison, Wis., May, 1975.

COLLINS, R. 1975. Conflict Sociology: Toward an Explanatory Science. Academic Press. New York.

COOLEY, C. H. 1910. Social Organization: A Study of the Larger Mind. Scribner, New York.

LEWIN, KURT. 1936. Some social-psychological differences between the United States and Germany. Character and Personality 4:278-308.

MEAD, MARGARET. 1935. Sex and Temperament in Three Primitive Societies. Morrow. New York.

PARSONS, T. R. F. Bales. 1955. Family, Socialization and Interaction Process. The Free Press. Glencoe, Ill.